The Pursuit of Happiness

John and Joy Kasson
1974

THE PURSUIT OF HAPPINESS

By Howard Mumford Jones

Cornell Paperbacks
CORNELL UNIVERSITY PRESS
ITHACA, NEW YORK

First published, Harvard University Press, 1953
First printing, Cornell Paperbacks, 1966

Library of Congress Catalog Card Number: 52-12265

PRINTED IN THE UNITED STATES OF AMERICA
BY VALLEY OFFSET, INC.
BOUND BY VAIL-BALLOU PRESS, INC.

To

MARK HOWE
who should have written it

Preface

I DID NOT THINK WHEN, some years ago, I found myself speculating on why the happy ending had diminished in American plays and novels, that the inquiry thus idly begun would lead me to consider such things as the burning of natural gas, the destruction of a library by Federal troops, the policies of the *Ladies' Home Journal,* the novels of Cooper, a small farm in Italy, and the right of a facial masseuse to pursue her calling in California. But past these and other oddities—for example, slaughterhouses in Louisiana—the trail has run, and I have tried to follow it. If the upshot of these intellectual adventures is a conclusion in which nothing is concluded, I can only say that if anything could be settled in the matter of happiness, it would have been settled long ago. *Vanitas Vanitatum*, exclaimed Thackeray at the end of *Vanity Fair,* which of us is happy in this world? Which of us has his desire? or, having it, is satisfied? But if I have faltered more or less in my great task of happiness (I wonder if anybody reads Stevenson nowadays), I hope at least to have been suggestive—to have opened up some vistas for the legal philosopher and for the historian of ideas as ideas have developed in these United States.

I should never have had courage to plunge into the tangle of court decisions or to work through one of the most amusing puzzles in my inquiry if it had not been for the enthusiastic support and selfless patience of Mark Howe. The dedication expresses not only my gratitude but my feeling that Professor Howe should have written this study. I owe particular thanks to Sterry R. Waterman and John H. Downs of St. Johnsbury, Vermont, for giving me the run of their law library, and to the staff of the St. Johnsbury Athenaeum, a library which, like many another modest New England institution, conceals unexpected treasures. The staff of the Harvard College Library proved unfailingly helpful; so were their opposite numbers in the Henry E. Huntington Library and the William L. Clements Library of American History. I am again indebted to Mrs. Greenough for the use of the notes of the late Professor Chester N. Greenough; and to Professor Ralph Barton Perry, Professor Maurice Mandelbaum, Professor Robert G. McCloskey, Professor Edmond N. Cahn, Professor Robert Wettach, Mr. Spencer Montgomery, and Professor Leonard Oppenheim for helpful suggestions. My wife has again been my best counselor.

I am grateful for the labors of Dr. John Pilkington, Jr., for checking my citations and for saving me from serious blunders. I am also indebted to the amused tolerance and indefatigable industry of the members of the seminar in American studies at Tulane University, who permitted me to inflict my hobbies upon them and who turned up many a gem of purest ray serene which I have shamelessly stolen in revising my book. They were Philip F. Detweiler, Albert L. Diket, Robert F. Gibbons, Charles W. Moorman, Albert H. Silverman, Thomas S. Kane, Howard A. White, and Thomas L. Wright.

These lectures were delivered on the Cook Foundation at the University of Michigan in January 1952. While I cannot hope to speak with the authority of my distinguished predecessors in this chair, nor adequately repay the kindness of the audiences and the hospitality of the Ann Arbor community, I can express my deep sense of gratitude for the honor done me.

In preparing this material for publication I have kept the lecture form, inasmuch as it is often difficult to translate words originally meant for oral delivery into the diuturnity of print. I have, I hope, acted within the spirit of the Cook Foundation in giving a thorough revision to the substance of what I then said.

Finally, I owe to Mrs. Jean Rideout of the staff of the Northwestern University Library a passage from a book by Charles Leslie, published in London in 1700, *A Defence of a book intituled: The snake in the grass,* which I quote here because it is too delightful not to be rescued from oblivion: "I must trouble the reader to correct the errata of the press, as he finds them. For I am quite tyr'd."

Howard Mumford Jones

Contents

But although a rational pursuit of personal happiness, if it were common, would suffice to regenerate the world, it is not probable that so reasonable a motive will alone prove sufficiently powerful.

Bertrand Russell

I

The Glittering Generality

In This Series of Lectures, I desire to consider certain implications of one of the best-known phrases in American history. That phrase is "the pursuit of happiness," as fundamental, as baffling, as confused, and as interesting an idea as ever appeared in a state paper. It is a notion impossible to define and difficult to forget. Of course, the pursuit of happiness is not an institution in the customary sense of institutions which the Cook Foundation exists to explicate, but the words appear in a basic American document and the concept underlies many of our activities in religion, government, education, business, amusement, and social psychology today.

Sometimes we do not see a continuing idea of this sort because of the transmogrifications it undergoes. A simple case of transformation appears in American religion. At the end of the seventeenth century the Rev. William Corbin, preaching about an earthquake, described it as an invitation to repentance and said that Christian reform would

> cause the Heavens to drop Fatness round about your Habitations, and the Earth to bring forth Plenty; and you shall not fail of abundance of all things for the maintenance of your Grandeur and comfort of your Lives. . . it will create health to your Bodies, quiet to your Minds, and add prosperity to all your Affairs; for God's blessing is all, and more than all this, to any People.[1]

Here is clear belief that Christianity can create happiness in the present world—on the familiar formula of *do ut des.*

[1] William Corbin, *A Sermon Preached at Kingstown in Jamaica, upon the 7th. June, Being the Anniversary Fast for That Dreadful Earthquake Which Happened There in the Year 1692* (New York, 1703), p. 14.

Yet about half a century later we find the more celebrated Jonathan Edwards defining happiness in quite another context. He said:

> The sight of hell torments will exalt the happiness of the saints forever. It will not only make them more sensible of the greatness and freeness of the grace of God in their happiness; but it will really make their happiness the greater, as it will make them more sensible of their own happiness; it will give them a more lively relish of it. . .[1]

Nowadays we are unlikely to agree that a more lively relish of happiness is to be got by safely witnessing as from a theater box the torments of the damned and are inclined to judge that happiness so described is no happiness at all.

But we have only to make a long jump to find that happiness has not disappeared from American religion. The kingdom of God was again brought back to earth by Washington Gladden and others when, at the opening of the present century, the movement known as the social gospel sought to forward Christianity here and now. As Walter Rauschenbusch wrote in *Christianity and the Social Crisis* (1907):

> The kingdom of God is still a collective conception, involving the whole social life of man. . . It is not a matter of getting individuals to heaven, but of transforming the life on earth into the harmony of heaven.[2]

"What is all the machinery of our industrial organization worth," asked Rauschenbusch, "if it does not make human life healthful and happy?"[3] and he answered his own question this way:

> If now we could have faith enough to believe that all human

[1] *The Works of President Edwards* (4 vols.; New York and London, 1844), IV, 276. The idea is at least as old as Tertullian.

[2] Walter Rauschenbusch, *Christianity and the Social Crisis* (New York and London, 1907), p. 65.

[3] The same, p. 370.

> life can be filled with divine purpose; that God saves not only the soul, but the whole of human life; that anything which serves to make men healthy, intelligent, happy, and good is a service to the Father of men; that the kingdom of God is not bounded by the Church, but includes all human relations—then all professions would be hallowed and receive religious dignity.[1]

Happiness remains a constant in these varying expressions of our religious faith.

If we turn to American education we can see the similar persistence of the idea. A little after the founding of the present government, in fact ten years after the ratification of the constitution, Samuel Harrison Smith of Philadelphia published his *Remarks on Education.* He argued that the end of learning is happiness, and he defined the happy man as follows:

> That man seems, on the whole, to be the most happy, who, possessed of a large stock of ideas, is in the constant habit of encreasing them, and whom every hour of his existence renders more informed.

He said that the sources of happiness in a republic were, in point of education, open to all:

> If happiness depends on improvement of mind and collision of mind with mind, [the] happiness of an individual will depend on general diffusion of knowledge and a capacity to think and speak correctly.[2]

This was in 1798. Within the last ten years Harvard College has published its much discussed *Report on General Education,* in which one will discover much the same philosophy, including the familiar plea to increase men's capacity for happiness by increasing their capacity to think

1 The same, p. 355.

2 Samuel Harrison Smith, *Remarks on Education* (Philadelphia, 1798), pp. 30, 39.

and speak correctly. This we now call "communication," but the purpose is the same.

If we turn to the theory of American government, we see another example of persistence. Let us go back to the original discussions out of which the American political philosophy arose. The purpose of government, said the Rev. Jonathan Mayhew in 1754, is evidently the happiness of men.[1] Ten years later the celebrated and erratic James Otis insisted that the end of government is "to provide for the security, the quiet, and happy enjoyment of life, liberty, and property."[2] This concept is Lockeian. Ten years afterward, in 1774, Josiah Quincy, Jr., stated that the object of civil society is "the greatest happiness of the greatest number," anticipating Jeremy Bentham by six years.[3] About ten years after the new century opened, Jefferson wrote a correspondent that the only aim of government is "to secure the greatest degree of happiness possible to the general mass of those associated under it."[4]

We all tend lazily to subscribe to what seems a platitude. But when the happiness of the mass of the people takes shape as the New Deal, the welfare state, socialized medicine, social security, or fair employment practices, bodies of solid citizens bitterly complain that we are drifting away from the primary purposes of government. Yet in his second inaugural address—the one which contains the famous phrase about one-third of the nation "ill-housed, ill-clad, ill-nourished"—President Franklin D. Roosevelt

[1] Jonathan Mayhew, *A Sermon Preach'd in the Audience of His Excellency William Shirley, Esq.* (Boston, 1754), p. 7.

[2] James Otis, *The Rights of the British Colonies Asserted and Proved* (Boston, [1764]), p. 14.

[3] Josiah Quincy, Jr., *Observations on the Act of Parliament Commonly Called the Boston Port-Bill* (Boston, 1774), p. 28.

[4] *The Writings of Thomas Jefferson,* edited by Andrew A. Lipscomb and Albert Ellery Bergh (20 vols.; Definitive edition; Washington, D. C., 1905), XIII, 135-136. Jefferson's letter, dated March 22, 1812, is addressed to F. A. Van der Kemp.

did no more than inquire what had happened to the original idea. "Have we reached the goal of our vision?" he asked. "Have we found our happy valley?"[1] The overtones of Rasselas in this phrase may have been good-natured irony, but F.D.R. was doing no more than reaffirming the theory of Locke, Mayhew, Otis, and the rest.

ii

If the idea of pursuing happiness is thus basic and pervasive in our cultural development, one ought, it would seem, to be able to define the idea, or at any rate to define what the Americans mean by happiness. Unfortunately the term belongs to a category of words, the meaning of which everybody knows but the definition of which nobody can give. The *New English Dictionary* learnedly tells us that happiness is "the state of pleasurable content of mind, which results from success or the attainment of what is considered good." Among theological writers relevant to American thought, Hooker is significant, and for Hooker

> happiness is . . . that estate whereby we attain, so far as possibly may be attained, the full possession of that which simply for itself is to be desired, and containeth in it after an eminent sort the contentation of our desires, the highest degree of all our perfection.[2]

If one looks in the latest edition of the great *Corpus Juris,* the law encyclopedia, one will read that happiness means "that more permanent enjoyment of life which attends on, and is almost identical with, welfare." I have observed, however, that what is intended for the welfare of an individual is not always regarded by him as synonymous

1 *The Public Papers and Addresses of Franklin D. Roosevelt,* edited by Samuel I. Rosenman (13 vols.; New York: Random House [and others], 1938-1950), VI, 4, 5.

2 Richard Hooker, *Of the Laws of Ecclesiastical Polity Book I,* edited by R. W. Church (Oxford, 1905), pp. 70-71.

with happiness, and I hope it is not too flippant to gloss these three sonorous statements as in effect defining happiness as wanting what you want and getting what you get and hoping that the two will coincide. He who endeavors to ascertain the meaning of happiness had better imitate the ingenious evasion of the problem in Johnson's *Dictionary,* where you will find happiness defined as felicity and felicity defined as happiness.

I lay some stress upon the imbecility of logic in this regard, because until one has hunted up what the saints and sages, the poets and philosophers, the thinkers and the wits have remarked about happiness, one can have no notion of the complexity of human desire. Horace, Disraeli, and Leigh Hunt agree that the basis of happiness is health; Rousseau found it to consist in a good bank account, a good cook, and a good digestion; Elbert Hubbard called it a habit; Stevenson says it is a duty; Santayana darkly remarks that happiness is the only sanction of life; and Longfellow (of all people!) wrote that to be strong is to be happy. If one believes poets as different in time, place, and interest as Edward Young and Amy Lowell, happiness is a state of being; but if one reads Thoreau, Epicurus, and Marcus Aurelius, it is a state of doing. It has been called a rare wine by Logan Pearsall Smith, a mere name by Robert Burns, and a woman by Friedrich Nietzsche. According to Hawthorne happiness is a butterfly which, when pursued, is always just beyond your grasp, but which, if you will sit down quietly, may alight upon you. David Hume said happiness consists of action, pleasure, and indolence; Juvenal equated it with the capacity to endure the ills of existence; and Swift declared it is the perpetual possession of being well deceived.

For one group happiness lies in social activity. That action is best, say Hutcheson and Burlamaqui, not to speak of Josiah Quincy, which procures the greatest happiness for the greatest number, an idea which descends from Richard Cumberland's *De legibus naturae* (1672) and looks forward to Bentham and John Stuart Mill. Paley thought happiness is the rule in society; and Corneille, Montesquieu, George Herbert, Bernard Shaw, Sir William Osler, Matthew Prior, and Victor Hugo agree that happiness exists only when it is shared. But a whole cloud of others are of quite opposite opinion and find happiness only by withdrawing from the madding crowd's ignoble strife—as, for example, Joseph Addison when he writes:

> True Happiness is of a retired Nature, and an Enemy to Pomp and Noise; it arises, in the first place, from the Enjoyment of ones self; and, in the next, from the Friendship and Conversation of a few select Companions. It loves Shade and Solitude, and naturally haunts Groves and Fountains, Fields and Meadows: In short, it feels every thing it wants within it self, and receives no Addition from Multitudes of Witnesses and Spectators.[1]

What may be called the individualistic or partitive concept of happiness as opposed to the social context received the endorsement of Carlyle when he said that "the only happiness a brave man has ever troubled himself with asking much about was happiness enough to get his work done."[2] Less acidly, Cicero, Burke, Bertrand Russell, and Ibsen placed happiness in tranquillity of mind; Shaftesbury and Mary Wollstonecraft, in the natural affections; Coleridge, Aristotle, St. Augustine, and Philo Judaeus in virtue; and Epicurus, William Cowper, Thomas à Kempis, Benjamin Franklin, and La Rochefoucauld in moderation. Perhaps the only sensible thing to do, confronted by

[1] *The Spectator,* edited by G. Gregory Smith (8 vols.; London, 1897-1898), I, 59.

[2] *The Works of Thomas Carlyle* (30 vols.; Centenary edition; London, 1896-1899), X, 156.

this diversity of views, is to applaud the statement of Archbishop Whately when he said that happiness is no laughing matter.

But whatever happiness has meant to these writers, happiness, in the American scheme of things, is a basic right; and we might begin our inquiry by tracing the history of happiness, the pursuit of happiness, and the pursuing and securing of happiness and safety as a fundamental constitutional element in our society. Let us briefly note that happiness does not appear as a basic element in the English Petition of Right against Charles I, in the British Declaration of Rights in 1688, in the statement about the inherent rights and liberties of Englishmen uttered by the Stamp Act Congress of 1765, or in the declaration of the First Continental Congress in October, 1774, which stood out for "life, liberty, and property."[1] We have to repair to Williamsburg, Virginia, in the spring of 1776 to see it emerge as unalienable.

iii

On Monday the twenty-seventh of May, 1776, Colonel Archibald Cary, chairman of a committee to prepare a new constitution for the commonwealth of Virginia, reported to the quite illegal revolutionary convention sitting at Williamsburg that the committee had drawn up a Declaration of Rights, "which he read in his place."[2] This declaration was read a second time at the clerk's table—a due formality—and was then referred to the committee of the whole. Reported back to the convention in June, this declaration unanimously passed its third reading on the twelfth of that month. On the fifteenth it was adopted. This paper was principally the work of

[1] "Declaration of Rights and Grievances, First Resolve," in Appendix C, *The Works of John Adams* (10 vols.; Boston, 1850-1856), II, 538.

[2] Kate Mason Rowland, *The Life of George Mason: 1725-1792* (2 vols.; New York and London, 1892), I, 229.

George Mason of Gunston Hall, near Alexandria, and was by him declared in a letter to George Mercer to be "the first thing of the kind upon the continent."[1]

Mr. Mason was an eighteenth-century *philosophe*. A member of the activist group that was steadily carrying Virginia out of the British empire, he participated in the intellectualism of the Enlightenment. At Gunston Hall he possessed a notable library, which, unfortunately, Federal troops destroyed when they occupied the country around Alexandria in 1862. They destroyed it for the reason that, not participating in the Enlightenment, they were unable to distinguish between George Mason, who died in 1792, and his grandson James M. Mason, of the team of Mason and Slidell. The disappearance of the library makes it difficult to know what authors formed George Mason's mind. However, in the admiring language of Kate Mason Rowland, George Mason's filial biographer, there is testimony from his writings and speeches that Mr. Mason was not only a classical scholar, but also a man possessed of a wide and solid reading in the literature of his own tongue. He was, in short, a worthy contemporary of Thomas Jefferson.

Mr. Mason had a particular view of what constitutes happiness. Writing some London merchants in June 1766 he had described himself:

> These are the sentiments of a man who spends most of his time in retirement, and has seldom meddled in public affairs; who enjoys a modest but independent fortune, and content with the blessings of a private station, equally disregards the smiles and favors of the great.[2]

[1] The same, I, 237. The letter is dated October 2, 1778. Inasmuch as the idea of natural rights was much bandied about among the patriots, I understand Mason to mean that his is the first formal declaration of rights to be embodied in an American constitution.

[2] The same, I, 130. The entire letter may be found in Appendix III of Volume I, pp. 381-389.

After his wife died he wrote that

> I determined to spend the remainder of my days in privacy and retirement with my children, from whose society alone I could expect comfort.[1]

He made his will, and in this document he enjoined his sons to

> prefer the happiness of a private station to the troubles and vexations of public business.[2]

All these passages point to the concept that happiness is chiefly to be found in retirement. But his will says something else to his children. The passage I have quoted continues:

> If either their own inclinations or the necessity of the times should engage them in public affairs, I charge them on a father's blessing never to let the motives of private interest or of ambition induce them to betray, nor the fear of dangers or of death, deter them from asserting the liberty of the country and endeavouring to transmit to their posterity those sacred rights to which they themselves were born.

Mr. Mason held a concept of public duty to which he was prepared to sacrifice his notion of private happiness; and though in making this transfer he created an irreconcilable conflict between the idea of happiness as a private affair and the idea of happiness as a social aim, he became the most influential spokesman for the idea of a declaration of rights including the right to happiness that the country has ever seen.

To a meeting of the freeholders and other inhabitants of Fairfax County in July 1774, Mr. Mason had presented a series of twenty-six resolves spiritedly asserting that the inhabitants of Virginia were not of the conquered but of

[1] Letter to George Mercer, October 2, 1778, in the same, I, 297.
[2] The same, I, 166.

the conquering and therefore to be treated on a footing with Englishmen. In the second paragraph of his resolutions one will find an important phrase about happiness:

> Resolved, That the most important and valuable part of the British Constitution, upon which its very existence depends, is, the fundamental principle of the people's being governed by no laws to which they have not given their consent by Representatives freely chosen by themselves, who are affected by the laws they enact equally with their constituents, in which . . . consists *the safety and happiness* of the community; for if this part of the constitution was taken away, or materially altered, the government must degenerate either into an absolute and despotic monarchy, or a tyrannical aristocracy, and the freedom of the people be annihilated.[1]

Here Mr. Mason, though his language is not crystal clear, seems to make the safety and happiness of the people tantamount to representative government.

In 1775, for the Fairfax Independent Company, George Washington commanding, Mr. Mason drew up another statement of principles, in which he asserted that

> no institution can be long preserved, but by frequent recurrence to those maxims on which it was formed

and said that

> we came equals into this world, and equals shall we go out of it. All men are by nature born equally free and independent. To protect the weaker from the injuries and insults of the stronger were societies first formed; when men entered into compacts to give up some of their natural rights, that by union and mutual assistance they might secure the rest; but they gave up no more than the nature of the thing required.[2]

[1] The same, Appendix VII, I, 419. My italics.
[2] The same Appendix IX, I, 430.

It is not clear how a natural right can be given up, but in this statement of equality we have the second element of Mr. Mason's political theory.

When the revolutionary convention assembled in Williamsburg in May 1776, it was natural that everybody should turn to so skilled a penman for a statement of basic principles. Unfortunately Mr. Mason suffered from that aristocratic disease, the gout, so that he did not arrive in Williamsburg until twelve days after the opening of the convention. Meanwhile Edmund Pendleton had offered a resolution declaring that the "United Colonies were absolved from all allegiance to or dependence upon the crown or the parliament of Great Britain,"[1] and this was adopted. But this bare statement was not philosophic, it did not appeal to the judgment of mankind. Accordingly a committee was appointed, consisting of Mr. Mason, Patrick Henry, and James Madison, charged with the duty of asserting the philosophic rights of the commonwealth of Virginia. This they did by reporting out Mr. Mason's declaration.

This statement, which Mr. Mason based largely upon his Fairfax resolves, consisted of fourteen articles, and though the committee and the convention meddled here and there with his language, the Virginia Declaration of Rights is essentially his work. The first paragraph reads that

> all men are created equally free and independent, and have certain inherent natural rights, of which they cannot, by any compact, deprive or divest their posterity; among which are the enjoyment of life and liberty, with the means of acquiring and possessing property, and *pursuing and obtaining happiness and safety.*[2]

[1] The same, I, 223. The literal wording runs: "declare the United Colonies free and independent States, absolved from all allegiance to or dependence upon the crown or parliament of Great Britain."

[2] The same, Appendix X, I, 434. My italics.

Mr. Mason has in this paragraph fused into a single whole the doctrine about happiness which he set forth in 1774, with a doctrine of natural rights which he set forth in 1775. His paragraph passed unchanged into the Virginia constitution of 1776 and, as we shall see, into many other state constitutions as well. The right to happiness, phrased by him as "pursuing and obtaining happiness and safety," was from the beginning of the revolution guaranteed to a large portion of the American people.

As all the world knows, the essence of what Mr. Mason asserted in Williamsburg in June was reasserted on an even more brilliant stage by Mr. Jefferson in July. An equally illegal Continental Congress was then meeting in Philadelphia. Its intentions were entirely subversive. To its wisdom Richard Henry Lee, another Virginian, on June 7, 1776, submitted a resolution declaring that the American colonies "are, and of right ought to be, free and independent states."[1] The pattern of events in Williamsburg was followed in Philadelphia. The naked resolution was adopted July 2, but it was again desirable to prepare a philosophic declaration for the benefit of mankind, and for that purpose a committee composed of Mr. Jefferson, John Adams, Benjamin Franklin, Roger Sherman, and Robert R. Livingston was instructed to prepare a statement. This statement was essentially the work of Mr. Jefferson.[2] On July 4, 1776, it was agreed to by the congress as the official statement of the principles upon which a new nation was being formed. The first section of the philosophical portion reads:

We hold these truths to be self-evident. That all men are

[1] *Journals of the Continental Congress: 1774-1789,* edited by Worthington Chauncey Ford (34 vols.; Washington: Government Printing Office, 1904-1937), V, 425.

[2] John Adams took a somewhat dim view of Jefferson's activity. See *Works,* II, 510-517. He admired Jefferson as a writer, but declared he was negligent in attendance.

> created equal; that they are endowed by their Creator with certain unalienable rights; that among these are life, liberty, and the pursuit of happiness.

Mr. Jefferson was even more of a *philosophe* than was Mr. Mason, though he was by no means a French *philosophe*. We know what was in his library, his papers have been preserved, and we know a vast deal more about his philosophic outlook than we know about Mr. Mason's. He has been made the subject of admirable studies by Chinard, Wiltse, Boorstin, Adrienne Koch, Malone, and others. Of Mr. Jefferson's general outlook the late Carl Becker wrote in his study, *The Declaration of Independence:*

> It was a humane and engaging faith. At its best it preached toleration in place of persecution, goodwill in place of hate, peace in place of war. It taught that beneath all local and temporary diversity, beneath the superficial traits and talents that distinguished men and nations, all men are equal in the possession of a common humanity; and to the end that concord might prevail on the earth instead of strife, it invited men to promote in themselves the humanity which bound them to their fellows, and to shape their conduct and their institutions in harmony with it.[1]

This is admirably said, and to the place of happiness in eighteenth-century America in the light of this philosophy we shall return.

Meanwhile, however, it must be observed that although Jefferson took over the doctrine of the moral sense from Hutcheson and others; though he accepted the not very illuminating formula of Gassendi, Wollaston, and Locke that happiness is the excess of pleasure over pain; though, as he wrote Henry Lee in his old age, "neither aiming at originality of principle or sentiment, nor yet copied from

[1] Carl Becker, *The Declaration of Independence: A Study in the History of Political Ideas* (New York: Alfred A. Knopf, 1948), p. 278.

any particular and previous writing," the Declaration "was intended to be an expression of the American mind"[1]—or, as he said on another occasion, the common sense of the matter—it is by no means easy to know what either Jefferson or the committee meant by the pursuit of happiness.

Young John Adams, for example, twenty years earlier confided to his diary that since we come naked into the world, increase in strength of body and mind but slowly, spend one-third of our time in sleep and three-sevenths of our waking hours in "procuring a mere animal sustenance,"

> if we live to the age of threescore and ten, and then sit down to make an estimate in our minds of the happiness we have enjoyed, and the misery we have suffered, we shall find . . . that the overbalance of happiness is quite inconsiderable [since] we shall find that we have been, through the greatest part of our lives, pursuing shadows . . . rather than substances.[2]

Here is young Benjamin Franklin, in his "Articles of Belief and Acts of Religion" (1728), taking a somewhat dim view of human perfectibility:

> when I stretch my Imagination thro' and beyond our System of Planets, beyond the visible fix'd Stars themselves, into that Space that is every Way infinite, and conceive it fill'd with Suns like ours, each with a Chorus of Worlds forever moving round about him, then this little Ball on which we move, seems, even in my narrow Imagination, to be almost Nothing, and myself less than Nothing, and of no sort of Consequence.
>
> . . . I imagine it great Vanity in me to suppose, that the *Supremely Perfect* does in the least regard such an incon-

[1] *Writings,* XVI, 118. The letter is dated May 8, 1825.

[2] *Works,* II, 20. See also II, 29, 65-66; and for his mature view a letter to Benjamin Rush, May 1, 1807 (IX, 593-594), in which Adams says that he and Rush have been engaged in building a palace of ice (i.e., public service) that was now melted away.

> siderable Nothing as Man. . . I cannot conceive otherwise than that he the *Infinite Father* expects or requires no Worship or Praise from us, but that he is even infinitely above it.

Even though Franklin goes on to remark that God will not be offended "when he sees his Children solace themselves in any manner of pleasant exercises and Innocent Delights," his general view is one of submission.[1]

Here is Mr. Jefferson himself writing John Page in 1763 that since "perfect happiness . . . was never intended by the Deity to be the lot of one of his creatures," resignation is the utmost man can attain:

> The most fortunate of us, in our journey through life, frequently meet with calamities and misfortunes which may greatly afflict us; and, to fortify our minds against the attacks of these calamities and misfortunes, should be one of the principal studies and endeavors of our lives. The only method of doing this is to assume a perfect resignation to the Divine will . . . by our uneasiness, we cannot prevent the blow before it does fall, but we may add to its force after it has fallen.[2]

These are, of course, the utterances of young men filled with eighteenth-century melancholy, but there is little in the later writings of the three to show that they essentially altered their philosophic attitude; and if we confine our views to the notion of private happiness held by a majority of the committee, we shall have to infer that in making the pursuit of happiness an unalienable right, they were

[1] *The Writings of Benjamin Franklin,* edited by Albert H. Smyth (10 vols.; New York and London, 1904-1907) II, 92-93; 94. For a characteristic expression of the mature Franklin see his letter to Priestley, June 7, 1782 (IX, 214), in which he wishes for leisure to study the works of nature, "I mean the *inanimate,* not the *animate* or moral part of them. . . the more I know of the latter, the more I am disgusted with them." Of course Franklin also preached cheerfulness even in the "Articles of Belief," but on this subject see below, Chapter III.

[2] *Writings,* IV, 10. The letter is dated July 15, 1763.

guaranteeing the American citizen the ghastly privilege of pursuing a phantom and embracing a delusion. We should, of course, turn to Locke, to Wollaston, to Adam Smith, to Hutcheson, even to Blackstone, whom Jefferson disliked but who nevertheless makes the pursuit of happiness the foundation of natural law, for a more political, a more social definition of happiness as a goal, but the disharmony remains; and if, in his first inaugural address, Jefferson could declare that "an overruling Providence . . . by all its dispensations proves that it delights in the happiness of man here and his greater happiness hereafter," he could also write Abigail Adams in 1817 that the Creator has so planned human life that "stealing from us, one by one, the faculties of enjoyment, searing our sensibilities, leading us, like the horse in his mill, round and round the same beaten circle," He lets this continue "until satiated and fatigued with . . . leaden iteration, we ask our own *congé*."[1] We shall return to this problem.

iv

The United Colonies became the United States of America, tied together under loose Articles of Confederation that were not so much a constitution as a treaty of alliance. Since a treaty is no good place for enunciating philosophic truths, no list of natural rights appears in the Articles of Confederation. However, new state constitutions were adopted by most of the thirteen colonies, many of them containing a bill of rights, including the right to happiness. The war ended, the Articles of Confederation proved unworkable, and by and by a constitutional convention met in Philadelphia to draw up and submit to the several states an instrument beginning: "We, the people of the United States." Mr. Jefferson was in France at the time, but Mr. Mason was a member of this conven-

[1] The same, XV, 96. The letter is dated January 11, 1817.

tion, and he did not like what it produced. Neither did Messrs. Yates and Lansing of New York, Mr. Gerry of Massachusetts, and a number of other delegates. Among other reasons for their distaste was the absence of a bill of rights from the new constitution.

The question of including such a declaration arose late in the life of the convention. Not until September was well along did Elbridge Gerry of Massachusetts propose, and George Mason of Virginia second, a motion to establish a committee to bring in a declaration of rights. The proposal met opposition. Mr. Sherman of Connecticut, sensing that the action meant delay, said a declaration was unnecessary, inasmuch as the state declarations were not repealed by the new constitution. Mr. Mason retorted that the laws of the United States were supposed to be paramount under the new document. When the matter was put to vote, there being but eleven states represented and the Massachusetts delegation happening to be absent, the motion was lost by a tie vote. The five states which opposed Mr. Gerry's motion were all Southern states including Virginia. This singular result was possible because, of the Virginia delegates, only Edmund Randolph associated himself with Mr. Mason, and they were outnumbered by Mr. Blair, Mr. Madison, and General Washington. One unhappy sequel of this split was the refusal of Messrs. Randolph and Mason to sign the new constitution.

The debate over adopting the new constitution shook the country in 1787 and 1788. The absence of a bill of rights was everywhere noted. Richard Henry Lee wrote Edmund Randolph that the lack of such a declaration left the new government "highly and dangerously oligarchic."[1] Elbridge Gerry wrote Samuel Adams that the

[1] *The Debates in the Several State Conventions, on the Adoption of the Federal Constitution,* edited by Jonathan Elliot (5 vols.; 2nd. ed.; Philadelphia and Washington, 1861), I, 503. See also pp. 492-494.

people were without security. Opposition in New York was so energetic that the eighty-fourth number of *The Federalist* was devoted to the ingenious arguments that since a bill of rights was originally an abridgment of prerogative, no abridgment was necessary when there was no prerogative; and that it would be dangerous to enumerate the rights of the people. Why declare that things shall not be done which there is no power to do? The Massachusetts convention ratified only by a close vote and after demanding, in fact, the addition of a bill of rights. The New York convention ratified by a slim majority of three, on the same implied condition. Maryland took much the same action. North Carolina would neither ratify nor reject, but Mr. M'Dowall declared in their convention that "a bill of rights ought to have been inserted."[1] But it was in Virginia that the argument was the hottest.

The convention met in June, 1788.[2] Mason, Henry, and James Madison were members. Mr. Mason became the chairman of the committee of opposition, and Mr. Henry became the leading orator of the committee. Time and again he demanded a bill of rights as "indispensably necessary"[3] to the constitution. Mr. Mason demanded such a declaration as a check to the general government and a safeguard to the people.[4] Letters from Thomas Jefferson to various Virginians were cited to the effect that Mr. Jefferson was opposed to the new document unless a bill of rights were added. Mr. Madison denied that this was what his friend Mr. Jefferson meant, and repeated the theory of *The Federalist* papers about such a statement.[5]

1 Elliot, IV, 210.

2 The most detailed account of this famous convention is found in David John Mays, *Edmund Pendleton* (2 vols.; Cambridge: Harvard University Press, 1952), II, chaps. xiii-xvi.

3 Elliot, III, 150; cf. pp. 138-139, 316-317, 445-449, 460-462, 578-589, 587-590, 622-625.

4 Rowland, II, 236; cf. Elliot, III, 265-266.

5 Elliot, III, 152-153; 199-200; 304, 314, 329-330.

In the end he won, but it was by the slender majority of ten in a convention of 168 members.

Nor was this total defeat for the bill of rights party. The two days following the vote ratifying the new constitution were given over to amendments to be proposed by Virginia, of which some twenty had been presented when the convention adjourned. Among these Mr. Mason's famous declaration had a foremost place, the leading paragraph being this familiar statement:

> That there are certain natural rights, of which men, when they form a social compact, cannot deprive or divest their posterity; among which are the enjoyment of life and liberty, with the means of acquiring, possessing, and protecting property, and pursuing and obtaining happiness and safety.[1]

In fact, an examination of the various bills of rights proposed by the several states interested in the matter shows that the right to happiness was commonly included in the amendments desiderated. One might therefore reasonably suppose that the right to pursue happiness would become part of fundamental federal law.

But an extraordinary thing happened. The new government did not get under way until April 30, 1789. On May 5 the House of Representatives received a communication from the Virginia General Assembly conveying the formal vote of that legislature demanding a federal bill of rights. Over a month went by. On June 8 Mr. Madison proposed that the Virginia bill of rights, including the right to happiness, be referred to a committee of the whole. This opened a long and inconclusive debate. The debate was resumed on July 21, and a committee of eleven was finally established. The committee did not report until the middle of August, and the report of the committee was not

[1] The same, III, 657.

accepted by the House until August 24. This report proposed the adoption of seventeen amendments. It went to the Senate the next day. Not until September 21, however, did the Senate accept the report of a conference committee proposing twelve amendments to the states, all that survived from 103 articles of amendment originally suggested by state conventions at the time the constitution was ratified. Small wonder that on September 29 Senator Grayson of Virginia wrote Patrick Henry:

> With respect to amendments matters have turned out exactly as I apprehended, from the extraordinary doctrine of playing the after game. The lower house sent up amendments which held out a safeguard to personal liberty in a great many instances, but this disgusted the senate, and though we made every exertion to save them, they are so mutilated and gutted that in fact they are good for nothing. . .[1]

The mutilation included the right to happiness. As originally proposed by James Madison the first amendment to the constitution was to read as follows:

> That there be prefixed to the Constitution a declaration, that all power is originally vested in, and consequently derived from, the people. That government is instituted and ought to be exercised for the benefit of the people; which consists in the enjoyment of life and liberty, with the right of acquiring and using property, and generally of pursuing and obtaining happiness and safety. That the people have an indubitable, unalienable, and indefeasible right to reform or change their Government, whenever it may be found adverse or inadequate to the purposes of its institution[2]

[1] William Wirt Henry, *Patrick Henry: Life, Correspondence and Speeches* (3 vols.; New York, 1891), III, 406.

[2] *The Debates and Proceedings in the Congress of the United States,* compiled by Joseph Gales [and others] (41 vols.; Washington, 1834-1856), I, 433.

But this vigorous language was shortened and softened by the House committee and then rejected by the House; and an attempt in the Senate to adopt language to the effect that "the doctrine of non-resistance against arbitrary power and oppression is absurd, slavish, and destructive of the good and happiness of mankind"[1] was rejected by that body. With these two votes happiness disappeared from the amendments and therefore from the federal constitution.

The twelve amendments were sent to the states, which eventually rejected two of them. In view of the vigor with which Mr. Mason, Mr. Henry, and others had declared that the country was done for unless a declaration of rights was immediately adopted, one might suppose that the first ten amendments would have been instantly agreed to. Not at all. Virginia, which had passionately demanded a bill of rights in 1788, lingered over the matter until December 15, 1791—that is, for two years—being the eleventh state to accede, and Massachusetts did not adopt the amendments at all, or rather did not vote until March 2, 1939, 150 years after the creation of the new federal government!

I suppose many citizens believe that Mr. Jefferson's phrase about life, liberty, and the pursuit of happiness was transferred to the constitution. This, of course, is not so. Nevertheless, in over a century and a half nobody has expressed dissatisfaction with the first ten amendments, and there seems to be no immediate movement to restore happiness to the federal government. Happiness, however, has not disappeared from constitutional law.

V

During the comprehensive discussion of the theory and practice of government in the last decades of the eight-

[1] *Journal of the First Session of the Senate of the United States of America* (New York, 1789), p. 124.

eenth century, it was more than once pointed out that some states had never adopted a declaration of rights. Colonial charters often guarantee to settlers the rights of Englishmen, but such a statement is not quite the same as a declaration of rights. Nevertheless, two of the original states—Connecticut and Rhode Island—were content to get along under their original charters until long after the present national government was created—Connecticut until 1818, Rhode Island until 1842. Even when Connecticut adopted a new constitution, it did not come out for happiness; and Rhode Island was content to make happiness an object of government but not an unalienable right. The early constitutions of six other original states—Delaware (1776), Georgia (1777), Maryland (1776), New Hampshire (1776), North Carolina (1776) and South Carolina (1776)—either included no declaration of rights or, if one was included, omitted happiness, or referred happiness to the preamble. The constitution of New Jersey (1776) and that of New York (1777) cited the text, or variants of the text, of the Declaration of Independence, including the right to pursue happiness. George Mason's language—the right to pursue and obtain happiness and safety—appears in the constitutions adopted by Virginia (1776), Pennsylvania (1776), Vermont (1777), Massachusetts (1780), New Hampshire (1784), and, in a sense, Delaware (1792), though the reading is importantly altered to:

> the rights of . . . enjoying and defending life and liberty, of acquiring and protecting reputation and property, and . . . of attaining objects suitable to their condition, without injury by one to another.[1]

So much for the fortunes of happiness among the revolutionary constitutions considered by themselves. But if one omits from the count colonial charters, enabling acts, tem-

[1] *The Federal and State Constitutions,* edited by Francis Newton Thorpe (7 vols.; Washington, 1909), I, 568.

porary instruments, what are known as "schedules," and organic laws for territorial possession, and also the constitutions adopted in or for the Confederate States of America; and if one counts the constitutions adopted since the Declaration of Independence, the American people have accepted about 120 state constitutions between 1776 and 1907, when Francis Newton Thorpe finished his great seven-volume collection of *Federal and State Constitutions* (Washington, 1909). When and how does happiness appear in these organic documents?

Happiness as an unalienable right has been of no concern at any time in this period to Connecticut, Georgia, Michigan, Minnesota, Texas, Utah, and Washington. It has been of intermittent concern in Louisiana, which in 1812, 1845, 1852, 1864, and 1879 did not think it worth while to enumerate happiness as an unalienable right, but in 1868 held that life, liberty, and the pursuit of happiness were fundamental, altered this in 1879 to "the enjoyment of life, liberty, and property," and in 1898 voted that the aim of government is to preserve the peace and to promote the "interest and happiness of the people." A Maryland constitution of 1776 says that non-resistance is "destructive of the good and happiness of mankind," but does not recognize happiness as unalienable. The state continued in this belief in 1851, declared in 1864 that life, liberty, the enjoyment of the proceeds of their own labor, and the pursuit of happiness were rights, and gave the whole thing up in 1867. Mississippi constitutions of 1817, 1832, and 1868 said nothing about happiness, but that of 1890 held that the people have a right to regulate, alter and abolish their constitution and form of government "whenever they may deem it necessary to their safety and happiness," provided the results were not repugnant to the federal constitution. The preamble of the New York constitution of 1777 refers to the action of the state assembly advising the creation of a government for the "happiness and safety" of the people and, as I have said, quotes the Declaration of Independence, but happiness disappeared from New York in 1821 and was not reinstituted in 1846 or 1894. In 1857 Oregon declared that government exists for peace, safety, and happiness. The state constitution of 1778 in South Carolina had no truck with happiness, those of 1790 and 1865 held that "peace, safety, and happiness" were objects of government, but in 1868 George Mason's phraseology briefly appeared only to disappear in 1895. In 1861 (1863) West Virginia omitted happiness, but in 1872 its citizens assured themselves of the right to pursue and obtain happiness and safety. Up to 1907 seven states have never plumped for happiness as an unalienable right, and the status of happiness has been of only occasional interest in six other commonwealths.

The guarantee of life, liberty, and the pursuit of happiness in the *ipsissima verba* of Jefferson appears in ten constitutions adopted by eight states, but this literal transfer does not appear until 1848 (Wisconsin). Life, liberty, property, and the free pursuit of happiness, sometimes altered to safety and happiness, are guaranteed in eleven constitutions adopted between 1799 and 1876 by five commonwealths. Like Maryland in 1864, Missouri in 1865 and again in 1875 guaranteed life, liberty, the gains of their own industry, and the pursuit of happiness to its citizens. Variants like "safety and happiness," "interest and happiness," "happiness and prosperity," "peace, safety, and happiness," and "protection, safety, and happiness" appear from 1777 to 1898 in Mississippi, Missouri, Montana, New York, Louisiana, North Carolina, Oregon, Tennessee, and Rhode Island, but not usually as fundamental rights. Other variants of Mason's phrasing, like "enjoying and defending" life and liberty in connection with happiness, or "enjoying" life, liberty, and the pursuit and obtaining of happiness also appear. Counting these, one finds the Mason formula in thirty constitutions adopted by seventeen states from 1776 to 1902. An interesting change to "acquiring, possessing, and protecting property and reputation" in association with the pursuit of happiness, the pursuit and obtaining of happiness, or the pursuit and obtaining of happiness and safety, has been found satisfactory in eleven other constitutions adopted by six states.

We are in a region where mathematics cannot help us, but that approximately two-thirds of the state constitutions adopted by the American people from the beginning of their independence to the beginning of the twentieth century have solemnly stated or guaranteed a right to happiness, or to pursue happiness, or to pursue and obtain happiness, or to pursue and obtain happiness and safety, or to pursue happiness in some other connection is a remarkable fact. It is likewise notable that many constitutions declare there is a popular right to alter or abolish a government which fails to secure happiness for the people. Finally, when concepts like life, liberty, property, reputation, safety, and security are enumerated in conjunction with happiness, the inference seems plain that those who wrote these constitutions felt it necessary to enumerate and distinguish happiness from a variety of other general nouns.

It is, of course, possible to echo the famous sentence of Rufus Choate, uttered in 1856, when he wrote of the "glittering and sounding generalities of natural right which make up the Declaration of Independence."[1] It is also possible to argue that when a declaration of rights appears in constitution A, it is merely copied from constitution B. Nevertheless, the glittering generalities persist; and if they

[1] *The Works of Rufus Choate*, ed. Samuel Gilman Brown (2 vols.; Boston, 1862), I, 215. From a letter to the Maine Whig Committee dated August 9, 1856.

are no more than a well-bred bit of constitutional decorum, it is perplexing that there should be so many variants among them. It is also interesting to note that the Congress of the United States, in acts admitting ten separate states to the union, has required, as a condition, that the state constitutions in question shall not be alien to the Declaration of Independence. For example, the act of April 19, 1864, admitting Nebraska, provides

> that the constitution, when formed, shall be republican, and not repugnant to the Constitution of the United States and the principles of the Declaration of Independence.[1]

Similar provisos governed the admission of Nevada, Colorado, North Dakota, South Dakota, Montana, Washington, Utah, New Mexico, and Arizona.

Perhaps the final commentary is Robert Frost's poem:

> That's a hard mystery of Jefferson's.
> What did he mean? Of course the easy way
> Is to decide it simply isn't true.
> It may not be. I heard a fellow say so.
> But never mind, the Welshman got it planted
> Where it will trouble us a thousand years.
> Each age will have to reconsider it.
> . . . .
> For, dear me, why abandon a belief
> Merely because it ceases to be true.
> Cling to it long enough, and not a doubt
> It will turn true again, for so it goes.
> Most of the change we think we see in life
> Is due to truths being in and out of favor.[2]

Whether happiness has been out of favor is an absorbing question. It is a question that has interested the courts.

[1] Thorpe, IV, 2344.

[2] From *Complete Poems of Robert Frost*. Copyright, 1930, 1949 by Henry Holt and Company, Inc., 75-77. Quoted by permission of the publishers.

They have deepened and sharpened our notion of many rights—that of liberty, for example, or the right to speak freely—and they have even struggled to define the right to pursue happiness. Perhaps the best way to begin finding out what Jefferson and Mason meant is to ask what the courts have said they meant.

II

As by an Invisible Hand

The late Chester Noyes Greenough once let fall some observations about the origins of the American Revolution that still sound their warning to the historian of ideas. He said:

> The amount of attention given to "Revolutionary" doctrine in the colonies must be very carefully weighed; it is certainly a mistake to imagine that the colonists brooded much over their wrongs and that long before 1775 there was a determined minority making for separation. It is, of course, true that if we pick out that particular strain from the rest, there seems to be a good deal of it . . . But when we take the whole mass as it poured out in pamphlets, magazines, sermons, newspapers, and all the rest . . . , the amount of writing in the Colonies that looks forward to anything like what occurred is exceedingly small.

This observation seems to me equally applicable to the student of the history of the unalienable right to happiness. Because of the importance of the Declaration of Independence, scholars have naturally desired to investigate its intellectual origins, and inquiry has pushed from the eighteenth century to the seventeenth, from the seventeenth to the high renaissance, from the renaissance to medieval scholasticism, and from the middle ages to antiquity. I do not deny the excellence of such research, to which I shall by and by gratefully return. But it is also true that the great mass of Americans have paid no attention whatever to this library of learning. Like Thomas Jefferson they have taken the Declaration and the right to pursue happiness as the common sense of the matter; and if, upon analysis, it is by no means clear what the common sense of the matter may be, they have on the whole been satisfied to let the phrase remain in convenient ambiguity.

Inasmuch as the right to happiness is guaranteed by fundamental documents, if we desire to comprehend the legal meaning of the phrase, we shall have to turn to the courts. But judges have likewise been frequently content to leave the idea in convenient obscurity. Of course it is not the business of the law to write a critical history of philosophy or of morals; nor is the duty of a judge to reason like a trained metaphysician. When court decisions have turned on the meaning of the pursuit of happiness, judicial dicta have therefore on the whole been confined to the common sense of the matter. Unfortunately in law as in epistemology the common sense of the matter is frequently a screen for a whole series of difficulties, and, as if conscious of this truth, some judges, in pronouncing on the right to happiness, have spoken as if they wished the wretched thing would quietly go away. A typical utterance in this regard is a decision of the Wisconsin Supreme Court in an inheritance tax case of 1906, when the bench remarked that

> the inherent rights here referred to are not defined, but are included under the very general terms of 'life, liberty, and the pursuit of happiness.' It is relatively easy to define 'life and liberty,' but it is apparent that the term 'pursuit of happiness' is a very comprehensive expression that covers a broad field.[1]

Comprehensive or not, the judges immediately identified the pursuit of happiness with the right to bequeath property, and in the light of this interpretation, proceeded to pass upon the constitutionality of the tax. I am reminded of an acid sentence by Mr. Justice Holmes in Noble State Bank *v.* Haskell: "Many laws which it would be in vain to

[1] Nunnemacher, Trustee *v.* The State, 108 NW 627.

ask the court to overthrow could be shown, easily enough, to transgress a scholastic interpretation of one or another of the great guarantees in the Bill of Rights."[1] But judges, as Henry Steele Commager observes, are in society, though insulated from it. We live under governments, he says,

> whose limits are set by courts, and with reference to intuitive ideas that find expression in the slippery phrases of due process, police power, liberty, public purpose, and so forth. Nor are these limits negative merely; the application of limitations is a positive act.[2]

The further observation of this historian that the judiciary sits as a perpetual constitutional convention redefining basic concepts and hedged by a divinity that can be questioned only by law school deans, is surely relevant to this case. The intuitive ideas of the Wisconsin Supreme Court led them to equate infringement upon happiness with an inheritance tax, conveniently forgetting that a rich man shall not enter the kingdom of God.

If the question of what the pursuit of happiness means in the courtroom is thus mystically determined, the historian is baffled by another element inherent in his materials. Nothing is more wonderful for most legal purposes than the reporting and indexing of cases decided in American courts. But as soon as one's inquiry ceases to be tech-

[1] Noble State Bank *v.* Haskell, 31 SC 186. Holmes's sardonic view of fine-spun theorizing again appears in an anecdote reported by Raymond Clapper: "One day a friend asked him if he had ever worked out any general philosophy to guide him in the exercise of the judicial function. 'Yes,' the aged jurist replied. 'Long ago I decided I was not God. When a state came in here and wanted to build a slaughter house, I looked at the Constitution and if I couldn't find anything in there that said a state couldn't build a slaughter house, I said to myself, if they want to build a slaughter house, God-dammit, let them build it.' " Quoted in Alpheus T. Mason, *Brandeis: A Free Man's Life* (New York, 1946) from the New York *World-Telegram* of May 22, 1936.

[2] Henry Steele Commager, "Constitutional History and the Higher Law," in *The Constitution Reconsidered,* edited by Conyers Read (New York: Columbia University Press, 1938), p. 236.

nical, the system breaks down. In the words of Professor Walton Hamilton of Yale,

> The headings are abstract concepts, verbal symbols, and legalisms. Records are not reported, and dates and occasions are swept away as of no account. Entries are set down as if the law were universal and unchanging; and holdings from a miscellany of times and jurisdictions are brought together to spell out a doctrine. The ghost of theology is still at large; and inconsistencies are leveled beneath the skills of the system-builder[1]

Difficult as it is in any body of materials to run down passages on so vague a concept as happiness, that difficulty is increased in the field of law by the fact that the indexing system points one way and one's interest moves in another. Consequently one cannot be sure that he has ascended to the original source of some striking interpretation of happiness, one cannot be certain that some decision, the main features of which turn on a technical legal rule, may not also have produced an interesting judicial dictum concerning happiness, and above all, one cannot know when an appellant has thrown in the right to pursue happiness along with any other sort of appeal in the general hope that something will stick, and when he really means that his right to happiness has been essentially jeopardized by the action complained of.

In the light of these observations it may be surmised that I have not surely discovered when the problem of defining happiness first appeared in an American court. However, two cases from the first half of the nineteenth century, though they are a good many years apart, illustrate the possible extremes of definition, since the first,[2] decided in 1810, turns upon the problem of happiness in

[1] Walton H. Hamilton, "The Path of Due Process of Law," in Read, p. 170, n. 3.

[2] Thos. Barnes *v.* First Parish, Falmouth, 6 Mass. 334.

the world to come, and the second,[1] which dates from 1855, is a vigorous explication of happiness here and now.

In May 1810 the Supreme Judicial Court of Massachusetts sat to decide an issue arising from the fact that church and state had not yet been fully separated in that commonwealth. Congregational ministers were still supported by public taxation; but the Rev. Thomas Barnes of Falmouth, a Universalist and a member of the unincorporated Universalist Society, nevertheless sued to get his salary paid by the town. The First Parish of Falmouth countered by the simple defense that the Congregational Society was the sole religious society recognizable under the law. The opinion of the court as delivered by Mr. Chief Justice Parsons equated happiness with Christianity, and not merely with Christianity but with Protestant Christianity, and not merely with Protestant Christianity but with the support of that church by Massachusetts.

His reasoning runs as follows: Since the constitution of Massachusetts declares that

> the object of a free civil government is the promotion and security of the happiness of its citizens,

and since

> these effects cannot be produced, but by the knowledge and practice of our moral duties, which comprehend all the social and civil obligations of man to man, and of the citizen to the state,

how is moral happiness to be obtained?

> To obtain that perfection, it is not enough for the magistrate to define the rights of the several citizens, as they are related to life, liberty, property and reputation, and to punish those by whom they are invaded. [Even] wise laws, made to this end, and faithfully executed, may leave the people strangers to many of the enjoyments of civil and

[1] Herman *v.* The State, 8 Indiana 545 (appendix).

> social life, without which their happiness will be extremely imperfect. Human laws cannot oblige us to the performance of the duties of imperfect obligation; as the duties of charity and hospitality, benevolent and good neighborhood; as the duties resulting from the relation of husband and wife, parent and child; of man to man, as children of a common parent; and of real patriotism, by influencing every citizen to love his country, and to obey all its laws. These are moral duties, flowing from the disposition of the heart, and not subject to the control of human legislation.

In fact, civil government would be extremely defective

> unless it could derive assistance from some superior power, whose laws extend to the temper and disposition of the human heart, and before whom no offence is secret.

Recognizing this truth, the people of Massachusetts, in no danger of choosing a false religion, inasmuch as Protestant Christianity of the Congregational sort lay plainly before them, made that church a "fundamental and essential part of their constitution."

> As Christianity has the promise not only of this, but of a future life; it cannot be denied that public instruction in piety, religion and morality, by Protestant teachers, may have a beneficial effect beyond the present state of existence. And the people are to be applauded, as well for their benevolence as for their wisdom, that, in selecting a religion, whose precepts and sanctions might supply the defects in civil government, necessarily limited in its power, and supported only by temporal penalties, they adopted a religion founded on truth; which in its tendency will protect our property here, and may secure to us an inheritance in another and a better country.

But what about Mr. Barnes, who, far from rejoicing in the immortal truth that Congregationalism protects property, complained that property was being taken away from him in the shape of taxes for a religion he did not believe, not to speak of the failure of the state to pay him an income comparable to that of his Congregational rivals? Mr. Barnes cannot complain. In the first place, nobody can compel him to become a Congregationalist; and in the second place, let him remember that he has to be governed by majority opinion. As for the complaint that it is intolerant to make Universalists pay taxes to support the Congregational church, the learned judge disposed of this by an astonishing piece of legal reasoning:

> . . . the object of public religious instruction is to teach, and to enforce by suitable arguments, the practice of a system of correct morals among the people, and to form and cultivate reasonable and just habits and manners; by which every man's person and property are protected from outrage, and his personal and social enjoyments promoted and multiplied . . . it remains for the objector to prove, that the patronage of Christianity by the civil magistrate, induced by the tendency of its precepts to form good citizens, is not one of the means by which the knowledge of its doctrines was intended to be disseminated and preserved among the human race.

In other words, Mr. Barnes had jolly well be happy in the fact that he lives among Congregationalists and not among cannibals. This astonishing *petitio principii* led Mr. Justice Parsons perilously close to saying that whatever is is right.

In his reasoning on the pursuit of happiness, Mr. Justice Parsons like Milton was content with nothing lower than

> that happy state
> Favored of Heaven so highly.

But my second specimen from the earlier nineteenth century is of the earth, earthy. In 1855 the Supreme Court of Indiana flatly declared that a state prohibition law was a gross violation of the right to pursue happiness. Asserting that the rights to life, liberty, and the pursuit of happiness existed anterior to the constitution, and, as it were, splitting the right to happiness into two parts—a right to enjoyment and a right to acquire and enjoy property—Mr. Justice Perkins delivered the opinion of the court which I quote *in extenso:*

> We lay down this proposition . . . as applicable to the present case; that the right of liberty and pursuing happiness secured by the constitution, embraces the right, in each *compos mentis* individual, of selecting what he will eat and drink, in short, his beverages, so far as he may be capable of producing them, or they may be within his reach, and that the legislature cannot take away that right by direct enactment. If the constitution does not secure this right to the people, it secures nothing of value. If the people are subjected to be controlled by the legislature in the matter of their beverages, so they are as to their articles of dress, and in their hours of sleeping and waking. And if the people are incompetent to select their own beverages, they are also incompetent to determine anything in relation to their living, and should be placed at once in a state of pupilage to a set of government sumptuary officers; eulogies upon the dignity of human nature should cease; and the doctrine of the competency of the people for self-government be declared a deluding rhetorical flourish. If the government can prohibit any practice it pleases, it can prohibit the drinking of cold water. Can it do that? If not, why not? If we are right in this, that the constitution restrains the legislature from passing a law regulating the diet of the people, a sumptuary law, (for that under consideration is such, no matter whether its object be morals or economy, or both,) then the legislature cannot prohibit the manufacture and sale, for use as a beverage, of ale, porter, beer, &c., and cannot declare those manufactured, kept and sold for that purpose, a nuisance, if such is the use to which those articles are put by the people . . . We think the constitution furnishes the protection. If it does not . . .

tea, coffee, tobacco, corn-bread, ham and eggs, may next be placed under the ban.

This court also cited scripture, but in a far different spirit from that of the Massachusetts case:

> It thus appears, if the inspired Psalmist (Psa. 104) is entitled to credit, that man was made to laugh as well as weep, and that those stimulating beverages were created by the Almighty expressly to promote his social hilarity and enjoyment. And for this purpose have the world ever used them, they have ever given, in the language of another passage of scripture, strong drink to him that was weary and wine to those of heavy heart. The first miracle wrought by our Saviour, that at *Cana* of *Galilee,* the place where he dwelt in his youth, and where he met his followers after his resurrection, was to supply this article to increase the festivities of a joyous occasion; that he used it himself is evident from the fact that he was called by his enemies a wine-bibber; and he paid it the distinguished honor of being the eternal memorial of his death and man's redemption.

Counsel had argued that the statute is justified on the ground that one man shall not injure another, but Judge Perkins swept this away in a single sentence.

> [This argument] is based on the principle that a man shall not use at all for enjoyment what his neighbor may abuse, a doctrine that would, if enforced by law in general practice, annihilate society, make eunuchs of all men, or drive them into the cells of the monks, and bring the human race to an end, or continue it under the direction of licensed county agents.
>
> Such, however, is not the principle upon which the Almighty governs the world. He made man a free agent . . . he put the apple into the garden of *Eden,* and left upon man the responsibility of his choice . . . He could have easily enacted a physical prohibitory law by declaring the fatal apple a nuisance and removing it. He did not . . .

> and he has since declared that the tares and wheat shall grow together to the end of the world.

Finally, returning from this excursion into theology, the court rested in political science:

> under our system of government, founded in a confidence in man's capacity to direct his own conduct, designed to allow to each individual the largest liberty consistent with the welfare of the whole, and to subject the private affairs of the citizen to the least possible governmental interference, some excesses will occur, and must be tolerated . . . The happiness enjoyed in the exercise of general, reasonably regulated liberty by all, overbalances the evil of occasional individual excess.

In Massachusetts Judge Parsons reasoned like the Roman curia; but in Indiana Judge Perkins seemed to represent the Abbey of Thélème. In the one decision it is the moral duty of the state to secure happiness for its citizens; in the other it is the moral duty of the court to resist the state in order that private happiness may not be disturbed.

ii

To pass from the 104th Psalm to the Fall of Adam, from the righteousness of Congregationalism to the righteousness of Adam Smith, and from Christianity to an abattoir is an astonishing step, but not more so than are other transitions in our story. The Slaughterhouse Cases of 1869,[1] 1872[2] and 1883[3] are notable in the history of jurisprudence for having wrenched the Fourteenth Amendment from the protection of Negroes to a problem in free enterprise, but they also represent a notable phase in the legal history of happiness.

In 1869 the Louisiana legislature, which, a product of

[1] 10 Wallace 273. This suit turned upon a problem of jurisdiction and is the least important of the three.

[2] 16 Wallace 36.

[3] 111 US 746.

the reconstruction years, was probably no better than it should be, granted the Crescent City Live-Stock Landing and Slaughterhouse Company, composed in fact of seventeen persons, the exclusive right for twenty-five years to build and operate a stock-landing place and slaughterhouse in the three parishes of which the city of New Orleans was the center. The right to create this monopoly was alleged to spring from the police power of the state. A thousand butchers were thus thrown out of work. Suit was therefore brought to break this monopoly, and reached the United States Supreme Court in 1872, a suit that, in the words of one commentator, had all the raw materials for a popular crusade inasmuch as

> a citizen had been enjoined from the sale of his land for a rival slaughterhouse; a like interdict had been laid upon a boatload of cattle headed for market by an unorthodox route; butchers who for years had done their deadly work were no longer free to follow their trade; and the local public was forced to have commerce with a monopoly or turn vegetarian.[1]

The court, by a divided vote, found for the Crescent City Live-Stock Landing and Slaughterhouse Company. But in 1879 an improved Louisiana legislature repealed the monopoly granted the Crescent City people and declared that the municipalities of the state had competent police power to regulate slaughterhouses. Under this dispensation the Butchers Union Live-Stock Landing and Slaughterhouse Company started to do business in New Orleans only to be sued by the old, original firm. The Butchers Union declared that the act of 1879 repealed the act of 1869, and, anyway, the legislature had no right to create a monopoly. The Crescent City people countered by contending that the act of 1879 was a breach of the

[1] Hamilton, in Read, p. 171.

legislative contract of 1869, and so the problem was again sent to Washington.

In the 1872 case brief for the plaintiffs was principally the product of John Archibald Campbell[1] of Alabama, a former justice of the Supreme Court (from 1853 to 1861) who had gone out with his state, an ex-Confederate who now argued for national sovereignty, a pro-slavery man who tried to throw around white butchers the protection presumably designed for the ex-slave. Mr. Campbell's brief was one of the most influential ever filed in the Supreme Court, inasmuch as the economic theory he advanced became the economic theory of the dissenting opinions in the 1872 case and of the majority opinion in the 1883 case, and thereafter standard economic theory in various American courts.

Mr. Campbell took a wide range. He quoted Thiers' *De la Propriété* to the effect that the right to one's self, to one's own faculties, physical and intellectual, one's own brain, eyes, hands, feet, in a word one's own soul and body, is an incontestable right, one of whose enjoyment and exercise by its owner no other person could complain, and one which nobody could take away. He then argued that the doom of Adam requiring him to earn his living in the sweat of his brow is a universal doom, but that the duty to labor, a thing ordained of God, secured a blessing to the whole human family. From these considerations he moved into history, declaring that this country was settled largely by Englishmen committed to free enterprise and the absence of all exactions by petty tyranny and of all spoliation of private right by public authority. He was opposed to monopoly. He held that slavery being abolished by the Thirteenth Amendment, the Fourteenth threw special federal protection around even butchers, inasmuch as the "privileges and immunities" therein guarded are

[1] He was associated in the case with J. Q. A. Fellows.

> the personal and civil rights which usage, tradition, the habits of society, written law, and the common sentiments of people have recognized as forming the basis of the institutions of the country.

In short, in the words of Professor Hamilton, this Alabaman resolved to use the Fourteenth Amendment, drawn to safeguard Negroes (the court said in its decision that "light comes" from the Civil Rights Act in interpreting the amendment and noted that this law was re-enacted after its adoption), to safeguard Southern whites, including their right to labor as both a liberty and a property. It is impossible, he thought, to sustain life, enjoy liberty, or pursue happiness if one is denied the right to work. The natural right to dispose of one's services became in his argument "freedom of contract" and it was this freedom of contract that the original Louisiana statute interfered with when it granted a monopoly.

The decisions of the learned justices in both cases particularly reveal the influence of Mr. Campbell's rhetoric. In the 1872 case, it is true, the majority opinion, delivered by Mr. Justice Miller, did not work its way from abattoirs to happiness, but this was done in the dissenting opinion of Mr. Justice Field and in the dissent of Mr. Justice Bradley, with whom Mr. Justice Swayne agreed. The Chief Justice, the Hon. Salmon P. Chase, also dissented. Judges on the minority side held that the Crescent City company had no claim in law, for the sufficient reason that they were interfering with the right of other Louisiana butchers to pursue happiness in their own peculiar way.

Mr. Justice Field thought highly of unalienable rights. Like everybody else in the case he referred approvingly to Corfield *v.* Coryell.[1] In that earlier case Mr. Justice Washington had had "no hesitation" in confining rights "to

[1] 4 Washington's Circuit Court, 380. This was, apparently, the leading case *par excellence* in the theory of rights.

those privileges and immunities which were, in their nature, fundamental," which it would be "tedious to enumerate," but which are comprehended under

> protection by the government; the enjoyment of life and liberty, with the right to acquire and possess property of every kind, and to pursue and obtain happiness and safety, subject, nevertheless, to such restraints as the government may justly prescribe for the general good of the whole.

This language was to re-echo in American courts thereafter.

Mr. Justice Bradley also referred approvingly to Corfield *v.* Coryell, to Blackstone, and above all to the Declaration of Independence, wherein, he said, was laid the foundation of our national existence, and wherein, to him at least, the "rights to life, liberty, and the pursuit of happiness are equivalent to the rights of life, liberty, and property." And he held that a law

> which prohibits a large class of citizens from adopting a lawful employment, or from following a lawful employment previously adopted, does deprive them of liberty as well as property, without due process of law. Their right of choice is a portion of their liberty; their occupation is their property.

This was because "the right to follow any of the common occupations of life is an inalienable right; it was formulated as such under the phrase 'pursuit of happiness' in the Declaration of Independence." "This right," he continued, "is a large ingredient in the civil liberty of the citizen" because it flows from "the fundamental proposition that all men are created equal."

However, Mr. Justice Bradley faced a dilemma. If all men are created equal, and if the right to pursue happiness is tantamount to the right to follow the common occupations of life, and if the legislature has no power to create a monopoly destructive of this equality, what right has an inventor to a patent or an author to a copyright in the pursuit of happiness, when such happiness clearly interferes with the happiness of others? And what about street-railway franchises, which, astonishingly enough, appear in his reasoning? "In such cases," he said, "a part of the public duty is farmed out to those willing to undertake the burden for the profits incidentally arising from it." He was clear that the pursuit of a franchise is part of the pursuit of happiness, just as much as is the patrimony of the poor man in his hands.

By such reasoning these justices worked their way from the curse laid on unhappy Adam to the happiness of street-railway franchises, best sellers, and the felicity of operating a slaughterhouse, all in the light of Mr. Campbell's famous brief. The minority of 1872 would have no truck with the metaphysical distinction by which the majority differentiated the rights of citizens of the United States from the rights of the citizens of any state and so left the Crescent City Live-Stock Landing and Slaughterhouse Company in happy possession of the New Orleans market.

By 1883, however, the composition of the court had changed, what had been bad law in 1872 had become good law, and the persuasive rhetoric of Mr. Campbell now achieved an even greater triumph. Mr. Justice Miller delivered the opinion of the court, in which the problem of the Fourteenth Amendment (and therefore of happiness) scarcely appears. But Mr. Justice Field wrote a concurring opinion[1] of very great influence, indeed. He returned admiringly to unalienable rights. These rights, he said, had never been more "happily expressed" than in the Declaration of Independence. There they are—clearly and beautifully put. They are self-evident truths—that is,

[1] Bradley, Harlan and Woods concurred with Field's reasoning, and Bradley reiterated his vigorous anti-monopoly doctrine of 1872.

truths recognized by anybody on mere statement. They are the gifts of the Creator, not the creation of emperors, or parliaments, or even acts of Congress. They cannot be bartered or given away or taken away except in punishment of crime. (But how, even if you are a criminal can you alienate what is unalienable?) To secure these rights governments are instituted. And if the government of Louisiana knew its business, which now at last it clearly did, it would protect the right of the Butchers Union Live-Stock Landing and Slaughterhouse Company to the pursuit of happiness. Was not a corporation a person in law—that is, almost a human being?[1]

> The right of men to pursue their happiness, by which is meant the right to pursue any lawful business or vocation, in any manner not inconsistent with the equal rights of others, which may increase their prosperity or develop their faculties, so as to give them their highest enjoyment

may not be jeopardized.

> The common business and callings of life, the ordinary trades and pursuits, which are innocuous in themselves, and have been followed in all communities from time immemorial, must, therefore, be free in this country to all alike upon the same conditions. The right to pursue them without let or hindrance, except that which is applied to all persons of the same age, sex, and condition, is a distinguishing privilege of citizens of the United States, and an essential element of that freedom which they claim as their birthright.

[1] In his minority opinion of 1872 Field had had to deal with Paul *v.* Virginia (8 Wallace 168), which held that a corporation being the special creature of a state could have no legal existence beyond the sovereignty which created it except as some other state might assent to recognize its existence. But this in effect was but to furnish a subterfuge for the Louisiana monopoly and, he said, "it is to me a matter of profound regret that its validity is recognized by a majority of this court, for by it the right of free labor, one of the most sacred and imprescriptible rights of man, is violated."

As he had in 1872, the learned judge turned to Adam Smith's *Wealth of Nations,* published in 1776, and cited Book I, chapter 10, to prove that the right of property is sacred and inviolable, and that the patrimony of the poor man lies in his hands. Perhaps in 1883 it did. It is, however, ironical that the index to the great edition of the *Wealth of Nations* edited by Thorold Rogers has no entry under "patent," none under "copyright," and none under "franchise," the nearest equivalent being a single paragraph in Book IV, chapter 4, on "premiums given by the public to artists and manufacturers who excel in their particular occupations."

However, in 1896 a third case from the same part of the world clinched the argument of Mr. Justice Field that

> It cannot be that a State may limit to a specified number of its people the right to practise law, the right to practise medicine, the right to preach the gospel, the right to till the soil, or to pursue particular business or trades . . .

In Allgeyer *v.* Louisiana[1] the Louisiana legislature was again interfering with the pursuit of happiness. It had passed a law imposing a fine on anybody in the state who

> does an act in that State to effect, for himself or for another, insurance on property then in that State, in any marine insurance company which has not complied in all respects with the laws of the State . . .

Had the statute been found constitutional, it would presumably have given Louisiana marine insurance companies a monopoly of Louisiana business. The Atlantic Mutual, of New York, had insured property belonging to a citizen of Louisiana, and when the Louisiana courts punished the Louisiana citizen for violating the act, the defendant appealed to Washington. Decision was given on March 1, 1897, by Mr. Justice Peckham, and again the

[1] Allgeyer *v.* Louisiana, 17 SC 427.

curse laid on Adam worked to protect the right to happiness. The court ruled that the Louisianan had a perfect right in New York to make contracts with a New York insurer without complying with Louisiana law, if his happiness and inclination so led him. Justice Peckham took a wide range. He referred approvingly to Mr. Justice Bradley's discussion of the right of the Butchers Union Live-Stock Landing and Slaughterhouse Company to pursue happiness by catering to carnivores. He, too, held that the right to happiness meant "the right to follow any of the common occupations of life." This is, he said, one of the privileges of the American citizen. He quoted with approval an opinion of Mr. Justice Harlan in Powell *v.* Pennsylvania to the effect that

> the privilege of pursuing an ordinary calling or trade, and of acquiring and selling property, is an essential part of his rights of liberty and property, as guaranteed by the Fourteenth Amendment.

Of course there is nothing in the Fourteenth Amendment about unalienable rights, unless these rights are transmogrified into the "privileges and immunities" which are there discussed; and the amendment, though it enumerates life, liberty, and property, says nothing at all about the pursuit of happiness. Indeed, if life, liberty, and the pursuit of happiness are unalienable, both Mr. Justice Peckham and the amendment are clearly guilty of tautology. The amendment declares that no state can deprive any person of life, liberty, or property, without due process of law. But if life, liberty, and property can be lost by due process of law, they are not unalienable rights. Mr. Mason's original language, however, is perfectly clear—there are certain inherent rights, of which men cannot, *by any compact,* deprive or divest their posterity—and Mr. Jefferson agreed with him. Obviously, however, you are not going to have due process of law until you have a society; yet society, according to the theory which produced these bills of rights, is the result of a compact. By no conceivable compact, however, can anybody divest himself or his posterity of any unalienable right. Finally, life, liberty, and property in the Fourteenth Amendment are not the same thing as life, liberty, and the pursuit of happiness, or, at least, they were not the same thing until, by going back to the Fall of Man, judges made them interchangeable by drawing the Fourteenth Amendment under the shadow of the Declaration of Independence and then inferring a definition of happiness as constitutional under a constitution which never mentions happiness. But perhaps Mr. Jefferson was at fault.

iii

The butchers of New Orleans seem to have awakened American litigants to the rich possibilities inherent in felicity. A right which had seldom vexed the courts before the epic battle between the Crescent City people and the Butchers Union Live-Stock Landing and Slaughterhouse Company was increasingly brought to the attention of learned justices. In the last sixty years the courts have been called upon to determine whether the pursuit of happiness as an unalienable right justifies opium smoking,[1] carrying a pistol,[2] the sale of liquor by municipalities,[3] the use of trading stamps,[4] the sale of contraceptives,[5] the spraying of citrus fruit,[6] the sterilization of imbeciles,[7] and the licensing of plumbers.[8] It has been

[1] Terr. Washington *v.* Ah Lim, 24 Pac 588.

[2] State *v.* Workman, 14 SE 9.

[3] Sheppard *v.* Dowling, 28 Sou 791.

[4] *Ex parte* Charles F. Drexel, on *habeas corpus,* 82 Pac 429.

[5] People *v.* Byrne, N Y Sup. Ct., 163 N Y Supplement 682.

[6] L. Maxcy Inc. *v.* Mayo, 129 Sou 121.

[7] State *v.* Troutman, 299 Pac 668.

[8] Scully *et al. v.* Hallihan, 6 NE 176. See also Schnaier *v.* Navarre Hotel and Importation Co., 74 NE 560; State *v.* Smith, 84 Pac 851; Burke *v.* Lynch *et al.,* 106 NE 976.

argued that to deprive a coal company of the privilege of paying miners in scrip is a violation of the right to pursue happiness.[1] Divorce from an epileptic[2] and the right of a Christian Scientist not to have his child vaccinated[3] have both been argued on this basis. The right of a reformed prostitute to privacy,[4] the right of a mortician to move his business from one city block to another,[5] the right to license fortune-telling,[6] and the right of a cleansing establishment outside the city limits of Defiance, Ohio, to do business in that municipality without posting a thousand dollar bond[7] have all been tested by the anterior right to pursue happiness.

In 1900 the Supreme Court of Illinois voided an act forbidding the use of the national flag in advertising (in this case, cigars) on the general principle that the pursuit of happiness permitted one Ruhstrat to use it if he wanted to.[8] On the other hand, when Mathew E. O'Brien sued in Connecticut to be admitted to the bar (because a committee of the county bar refused to license him), the Supreme Court of Errors in that state, in 1906, though it admitted the unalienable right of every American to follow "any of the common industrial occupations," denied Mr. O'Brien's petition on the ground that, however happy it might make him to practice law, he was "seeking to obtain a right of property which he has not got."[9] And in Kentucky in 1909 the spirit of Mr. Justice Perkins of Indiana reappeared in Commonwealth *v.* Campbell, when the

[1] State *v.* Peel Splint Coal Co., 15 SE 1000.

[2] Gould *v.* Gould, 61 Atl 604.

[3] Cram *v.* Schoolboard of Manchester, 136 Atl 263.

[4] Melvin *v.* Reid *et al.*, 297 Pac 91.

[5] Brown *v.* City of Los Angeles, 192 Pac 716.

[6] Davis *v.* State, 160 NE 473.

[7] Myers D B A Myers Cleaners of Delphos, Ohio, *v.* City of Defiance, 36 NE 2d 162.

[8] Ruhstrat *v.* People, 57 NE 41.

[9] *In re* O'Brien's Petition, 63 Atl 777.

Court of Appeals voided a municipal ordinance forbidding the bringing of liquor into Nicholasville, Kentucky. After quoting Blackstone, Judge Cooley, and J. S. Mill, the court spiritedly remarked that

> Under our institutions there is no room for that inquisitorial and protective spirit which seeks to regulate the conduct of men in matters in themselves indifferent, and to make them conform to a standard not of their own choosing, but the choosing of the lawgiver; that inquisitorial and protective spirit which seeks to prescribe what a man shall eat and wear, or drink or think, thus crushing out individuality and insuring Chinese inertia by the enforcement of the use of the Chinese shoe in the matter of the private conduct of mankind.[1]

Judges have argued for the moral right of the state to compel citizens to be happy, or at least to impel them away from unhappiness; and they have with equal fervor denounced the state for officiously interfering with the private happiness of individuals. They have denounced private individuals for wasting the resources of the commonwealth in their selfish pursuit of happiness, and they have reprimanded the state for interfering in the private and self-regarding pursuit of happiness by individuals. However amusing and contradictory their decisions may be, one common element tends to bind them together in the decades following upon the last of the slaughterhouse cases; namely, the equating of freedom of contract and freedom to labor with the right to pursue happiness.

[1] Commonwealth *v.* Campbell, 117 SW 383. "The Bill of Rights, which declares that among the inalienable rights possessed by the citizens is that of seeking and pursuing their safety and happiness, and that the absolute and arbitrary power over the lives, liberty, and property of freemen exists nowhere in a republic, not even in the largest majority, would be but an empty sound if the Legislature could prohibit the citizens the right of owning and drinking liquor, when in so doing he did not offend the laws of decency by being intoxicated in public." See also *Ex parte* Wilson, 119 Pac 596, which depends upon this case.

The rule has not only been applied in cases[1] involving conspiracy or monopoly in restraint of trade; it has been used to question or void statutes, the effect of which has been to prohibit private banking,[2] laws forbidding the discharge of a workman because he is a member of a union,[3] and taxes on merchants using trading stamps.[4] In a complex Nevada case of 1910 the court said:

> Most people rely for a living upon the pursuit of their ordinary avocations, and the most affluent are dependent in a large degree upon these. Comparatively few are possessed of such means that they will not need to labor or engage in the ordinary business callings. It would not be creditable for these favored ones, while young and strong, to idle away their time and live as drones upon the world. But, regardless of them, how are the great masses of the people to acquire property, pursue happiness and enjoy life and liberty unless they are permitted to engage in the ordinary avocations which are not injurious in themselves, and are beneficial to the individual and the community? It is quite as important that the people be free to enter these callings, and by their labor or investment of money or use of property which will enable them to obtain safety from want and acquire happiness as that the vested rights of the wealthy be protected. Any attempt of the Legislature to prohibit the pursuit of these harmless and useful avocations, or to restrict them further than necessary for the protection of the public, is an encroachment upon the liberty and just rights of the citizen. If this act [a statute requiring banks to be corporations licensed by the state banking board] can be held a valid exercise of legislative power, other laws may be passed and sustained on the grounds urged in support of this statute, which would be a dis-

1 Walsh *v.* Association of Master Plumbers of St. Louis, Mo., 71 SW 454; US *v.* Morris, 125 Fed 322; Territory *v.* Long Bell Lumber Co., 99 Pac 911; Denver Jobbers Association *v.* People, 122 Pac 404.

2 State *v.* Scougal, 51 NW 858; First State Bank *v.* Shallenberger, 172 Fed 1001; Marymont *v.* Nevada State Banking Board, 111 Pac 295.

3 State *v.* Kreutzberg, 90 NW 1098.

4 Humes *v.* City of Little Rock, 138 Fed 929.

> credit to a czar or absolute potentate, and which in the face of the constitutional provisions for the protection of the citizen secured by the blood of our forefathers would deny to the people the right to pursue honest, beneficial, and ordinary callings, and result in their injury and distress. That incomparable judge of the human heart and mind said: "You take my life when you take the means whereby I live."[1]

If a quotation from Shylock is a somewhat odd way of supporting judicial tenderness for the morals of the children of wealth, let us listen to a Wisconsin court defending the right of an employer to fire anybody he pleases:

> As each morning comes, the employé is free to decide not to work, the employer not to receive him, but for this statute [providing that nobody shall be discharged because he is a member of a union] . . . the act . . . invades the liberty of the employer in an extreme degree, and in a respect entitled to be held sacred except for the most cogent and countervailing considerations . . . Hardly any of the personal civil rights is higher than that of free will in forming and continuing the relation of master and servant. If that may be denied by law, the result is legalized thraldom, not liberty.

It is perhaps significant that Mr. Justice Dodge, the author of this remarkable paragraph, also declared in the same decision that words like life, liberty, and the pursuit of happiness "are not to be taken in their absolute sense."[2] Here is Mr. Justice Williams of Arkansas determined to stop the taxing of merchants who use trading stamps:

> The freedom of labor is perhaps the most sacred of all those [rights] that are guarantied by the national and state Constitutions. A man has the right to earn his livelihood and support his family by following any vocation not

[1] Marymont *v.* Nevada State Banking Board, 111 Pac 295.
[2] State *v.* Kreutzberg, 90 NW 1098.

> harmful to society. It is not sufficient that it may seem useless to the court. Things that are useless to one man are articles of prime necessity to another. To be within the legislative power of suppression, an occupation must be deleterious in its nature, or likely to become so, such as theaters and public balls, which, without police supervision, are apt to degenerate into indecency and riot. A large part of the pursuits of life are not of apparent utility, do nothing to secure food, shelter, or clothing to mankind, yet they assist some in that pursuit of happiness which the Declaration of Independence proclaims to be one of the inalienable rights of man.[1]

What, one is inclined to inquire, has become of the doctrine that the patrimony of the poor man is in his hands? When Paulina Feingold was had up in Connecticut for selling goods without a license as an itinerant vendor, the court held that she might reasonably be fined for not having deposited $500 with the proper state official, since the legislature may require a guaranty that an itinerant vendor shall not employ the "peculiar elements" of his trade for purposes of fraud—though no fraud was shown![2] Yet the next year, in the neighboring state of New York, the Court of Appeals declared:

> There is no more sacred right of citizenship than the right to pursuit unmolested a lawful employment in a lawful manner. It is nothing more nor less than the sacred right of labor. All laws, therefore, which impair or trammel these rights, which limit one in his choice of a trade or a profession, or confine him to work or live in a specified locality, or exclude him from his house, or restrain his otherwise lawful movements, are infringements upon his fundamental rights of liberty.[3]

1 Humes *v.* City of Little Rock, 138 Fed 929.

2 State *v.* Feingold, 59 Atl 211.

3 Schnaier *v.* Navarre Hotel and Importation Co., 74 NE 560. See in this connection the dissenting opinions of Campbell, J., and Morse, J., in People *v.* Phippin, 37 NW 888.

It would be difficult to demonstrate that itinerant vendors are either more or less likely to commit fraud than are private bankers, even in a world in which courts have vigorously denounced the state regulation of private banking and with equal sincerity upheld the licensing of peddlers.

iv

In later years, however, there has been a tendency not to confine the inalienable right to happiness to the pursuit of one's calling, but to take a wider range. Two cases from the Pacific coast beautifully illustrate the later proliferations and polarities of the happiness principle. One is from the 1890's, the other was decided in 1941, and the lapse of fifty years reveals an unexpected degree of flexibility in the judicial theory of happiness. The earlier case,[1] from the then Territory of Washington, concerns one Ah Lim, a Chinese, who was caught smoking opium, and who proved to be of intense interest to the Supreme Court of that territory, which had a good deal of difficulty making up its collective mind about the legality of his conviction. Ah Lim sued on the ground that a territorial statute depriving him of the right to smoke opium was an unwarrantable violation of his right to life, liberty, and the pursuit of happiness "through a limitation upon the means and ways of enjoyment," and his plea was heard with sympathy by Mr. Justice Scott, who found the law thoroughly unconstitutional:

> here a single inhalation of opium, even by a person in the seclusion of his own house, away from the sight, and without the knowledge of any other person, constitutes a criminal offence . . . regardless of the actual effect of the particular act upon the individual . . .

[1] Terr. Washington *v.* Ah Lim, 24 Pac 588.

Even if

> society has an interest in the promotion and preservation of the bodily, mental, and moral health of each individual citizen . . . it cannot be that every self-regarding act of the person which the legislature may choose to prohibit upon the ground that it is injurious to the individual, and thereby to the state, must be allowed to stand unquestioned through the courts . . .

He did not question that

> the habit of smoking opium may be repulsive and degrading; that its effects would be to shatter the nerves, and destroy the intellect . . . But there is a vast difference between the commission of a single act and a confirmed habit.

The act seemed to him an extreme new step in government, an unconstitutional step, and he said so. But he could not persuade his colleagues, who took what I can only characterize as a flippant attitude toward the bill of rights.

For the majority opinion ran to the effect that

> It is common to indulge in a great deal of loose talk about natural rights and liberties, as if these were terms of a well-defined and unchangeable meaning. There is no such thing as an absolute or unqualified right or liberty guarantied to any member of society . . . The natural rights of the subject, or his rightful exercise of liberty in the pursuit of happiness, depends [*sic*] largely upon the amount of protection which he receives from the government.

Such language, it is obvious, arbitrarily reverses the whole theory of a bill of rights by the simple process of substituting the word "relative" for "absolute," and the paternal state for the compact theory of society. The majority opinion was unabashedly revolutionary in this sense. The moral indignation of the court was aroused by opium smoking, of which it said:

> It is a matter of general information that it is an insidious and dangerous vice, a loathsome, disgusting, and degrading habit, that it is becoming dangerously common with the youth of the country, and that its usual concomitants are imbecility, pauperism, and crime.

So far as I can discover, no testimony of this sort was before the court, but on the theory that "there ought to be a law," the bench propounded a doctrine under which, as I make it out, the commonwealth could do pretty much as it pleased. The court said:

> . . . the state has an interest in the intellectual condition of each of its citizens, recognizing the fact that society is but an aggregation of individuals, and that the moral or intellectual plane of society is elevated or degraded in proportion to the plane occupied by its individual members, and that the education is not compelled for the benefit of the child during its minority, or for its exclusive benefit after its majority. The state has an undisputed right to, and does, provide gymnasium attachments to its schools. . . The object. . . is not. . . the exclusive benefit of the child. The state has an interest in the health of its citizens, and has a right to see that its citizens are self-supporting. . . If the state concludes that a given habit is detrimental to either the moral, mental, or physical well-being of one of its citizens, to such an extent that it is liable to become a burden upon society, it has an undoubted right to restrain the citizen from the commission of that act; and fair and equitable consideration of the rights of other citizens, make[s] it not only its right, but its duty, to restrain him.

In fact, the court held that if a man maims himself so as to become a public charge, "no one will doubt the right of the state to punish him." I think it is not too severe a gloss upon this extravagant language to observe that if the intent of the original bills of rights was to protect the individual against his enemy, the state, the language of the court in Washington *v.* Ah Lim implies that the state has a moral duty to protect itself against its enemy, the individual.

Fifty years later the Fourth Appellate Court of California reverted, in an amusing opinion,[1] to sounder doctrine. Miss Helen Whitcomb of Massachusetts had gone to California to continue her occupation of massaging the face, only to have the state board of cosmetology clamp down upon her for operating without a license. The license required that she pass examinations in various matters, including the art of hair-dressing, albeit she presented testimony in the lower court that a facial masseuse did not disturb anybody's permanent wave. The court held that her own right to pursue happiness and to increase the happiness of others was paramount to any such unreasonable interference by the state. Judge Kelly delivered the opinion, which runs in part as follows:

> We must assume that the desire and inclination of mankind to adorn and beautify the person is not wicked or evil of itself. From earliest ages the practice of personal adornment, particularly by the fair sex, has been indulged, as evidenced by the ancient Egyptian tombs, and this with the approval and even the applause of the sterner sex. The noblest epic in all literature glorifies the deeds of heroes on the windy plains of Troy, contending for the glamorous Helen of Sparta. . . Following the ancient tradition of her sex, the modern dame or damsel, viewing with dismay the incipient extra chin or tiny crowfoot, marking the plodding progress of Father Time, is impelled to erect bunkers of defense armed to withstand the inevitable assault. All of this is lawful and within the realm of inalienable rights classically defined as the "pursuit of happiness." If, then, it is lawful for all to endeavor to preserve or to regain those treasured charms of yesteryear, it must also fall within the legal protection of the constitutional guarantees for those

[1] Helen Walker Whitcomb *v.* Katherine E. Emerson *et al.,* 115 Pac 892.

> skilled in appropriate arts to serve the needs of those who seek the enhancement or preservation of personal beauty, subject only to the right of the state to impose such reasonable regulations as will protect the health, safety, morals, and general welfare of the public.

But was the examination required by the state board of cosmetology such a reasonable regulation? The court said, no. As a masseuse Miss Whitcomb

> sustains herself abundantly and desires to continue to be self-sustaining. . . an ambition in this day not wholly without need of encouragement. . . in order to secure her right to labor as she chooses she must become a "hairdresser" in fact and to that end practice, have experience in, and pass an examination in shampooing, waving, coloring, dressing and care of the hair, or in the alternative, starve or go to jail. We can find nothing in the relation of facial massage with the arts of hair-dressing which suggests that the public morals, safety, health or general welfare demands that the masseuse must be trained in those arts. We consider the attempted relation of hair-dressing and facial massage arbitrary in the extreme. Viewing the varying modes of hairdressing over a span of fifty years it may be said that such art is more akin to architecture than to the care of the skin.

And with this masculine snort the court set Miss Whitcomb free.

The right to pursue happiness is clearly a vague sort of thing. Why is it no infringement of that right to license fortune-tellers, but a clear infringement to license photographers?[1] Why is it unconstitutional for a man in Indiana to waste natural gas, which is his property[2] but constitutional in Idaho to sterilize one Troutman on the ground that it is no invasion of his right to pursue happiness and

[1] State *v.* O. G. Cromwell, 9 NW 2d 914.

[2] Townsend *v.* State, 47 NE 19. See also Commonwealth *v.* Trent *et al.*, 77 SW 390.

safety?[1] Why is freedom of contract made synonymous with the pursuit of happiness when, as Mr. Justice Stone remarked in Morehead *v.* New York,[2]

> There is grim irony in speaking of the freedom of contract of those who, because of their economic necessities, give their services for less than is needful to keep body and soul together.

Or why, in Nunnemacher, Trustee, *v.* The State,[3] did the Wisconsin Supreme Court equate happiness with property?

> To deny that there is such a universal desire, or to deny that the fulfillment of this desire contributes in a large degree to the attainment of human happiness, is to deny a fact as patent as the shining of the sun at noonday. And so we find that, however far we penetrate into the history of the remote past, this idea of the acquisition and undisturbed possession of private property has been the controlling idea of the race, the supposed goal of earthly happiness.

The court then cited the Old Testament to prove that Mosaic law bristled with provisions recognizing the right of inheritance. Presumably the court had in mind the King James Bible. According to Young's *Concordance* the word "happy" or "happiness" occurs in the Old Testament seventeen times, but in no case does happiness refer to property, but to life wisely lived according to the precepts of the Almighty—for example, "Happy is he that hath the God of Jacob for his help, whose hope is in the Lord his God" (Psalm 146: 15).

The theory of happiness as an unalienable right antedates the American judicial system. If the courts have struggled to adapt an eighteenth-century concept to modern times, it may be that their confusion has in part been caused by their failure to study the history of the ways by

[1] State *v.* Troutman, 299 Pac 668.
[2] Morehead *v.* New York *ex rel.* Tipaldo, 56 SC 918.
[3] Nunnemacher, Trustee *v.* The State, 108 NW 627.

which this influential concept became central in American political and cultural thinking. It will at any rate be useful to inquire what streams of thought, what ethical and philosophic tendencies were at work to create in the eighteenth century a legal phrase so baffiing in its implications today, albeit it seemed to Jefferson and his contemporaries merely the common sense of the matter. Why should the common sense of the matter produce these contradictory glosses on the right to pursue happiness or to pursue and obtain happiness? Let us return once more to the eighteenth century.

III

Our Being's End and Aim

We have now reviewed the curious history of the concept of a bill of rights (including the right to happiness) in our political development, and we have inquired of the courts what in their opinion is the legal meaning of the right to pursue, or to pursue and obtain, felicity. I call the political history curious because, if a bill of rights is a statement of fundamental political axioms, one might expect it to appear universally in our constitutions, whereas its appearance is intermittent and, concomitantly, a statement of the right to pursue happiness is still more unpredictable. Nevertheless, among the state constitutions the right to pursue and obtain happiness alone or in conjunction with some other goal does appear; and courts, including federal courts, have had to deal with this elusive concept.

But it is difficult to ascertain what the pursuit of happiness means in law. In one case the pursuit of happiness implies happiness in the world to come; in another, it is happiness here and now, with no reference to felicity hereafter. A large number of decisions (especially in the later nineteenth century) assume that the pursuit of happiness is tantamount to freedom of contract; and the practical result of this reasoning has been to prevent the state from regulating hours of labor or the payment of wages in scrip or the issuance of trading stamps, although the intent of such legislation was the happiness of society. Still other decisions reverse this interpretation and in forbidding an individual to smoke opium or burn natural gas day and night or sell a book entitled *What Every Young Girl Should Know,*[1] deny the individual the right to these particular enjoyments or interests. The basis of the right to happiness in the minds of some judges—for example, when the constitutionality of an inheritance tax is concerned—is found in divine law as expressed in the Bible; but the sincere faith of a believer in the tenets of Christian Science did not persuade the court that in refusing to allow his child to be vaccinated, he was not violating the law. Nor can any legal preference for the Bible as against *Science and Health; with Key to the Scriptures* be read into this decision.

Happiness has sometimes been made synonymous with the public welfare, and sometimes with the right of the individual to be protected against the public—for example, in the case of a motion picture based on the public records of a murder trial in California.[2] In sum, the concept of an unalienable right to the pursuit of happiness seems to lie in a twilight zone, admirably delimited in a paragraph from a decision by the Supreme Court of Florida dealing with the power of the state to forbid the use of arsenical spray on citrus fruit. The court had previously declared that the fundamental rights to life, liberty, property, and the pursuit of happiness must not be infringed; then, in a cloud of rhetoric such as the contemplation of ultimates usually creates in the judicial mind, it went on to say:

> And since the supposed promotion of the public welfare has almost invariably been the excuse for all the arbitrary and unjustifiable deprivations of life, liberty and property which have heretofore been committed, from the time pagan Emperors burned Christian martyrs in the imperial amphitheatre at Rome to the date of the rendition of this opinion [1931], the justification under our constitutional

1 See, for this, People *v.* Byrne, N.Y. Sup. Ct., 163 N.Y. Supplement 682.
2 Melvin *v.* Reid, 297 Pac. 91.

> system for enacting laws interfering with property rights and individual freedom must be shown to rest upon considerations greater than the alleged promotion of the general welfare alone.[1]

Precisely. But you will observe that the right to pursue happiness has quietly disappeared from this sentence, or rather has become the right to acquire property; and also that "considerations greater than the alleged promotion of the general welfare alone" are the point at issue in any definition of happiness.

Since judges disagree, let us retrace our footsteps to the year 1776, and inquire of Jefferson's generation what they meant by happiness. Like the courts we are confronted with ultimates, and I have already remarked on the difficulty of studying so vague a word. Almost every conceivable system of human thought has touched in some manner upon the notion of felicity, whether flatly to deny its possibility with the extreme pessimists, or with the extreme mystics, to find perfect happiness in an immediate, supranormal communion with deity. A history of happiness would be not merely a history of mankind, but also a history of ethical, philosophic, and religious thought.

Nevertheless, our inquiry is pragmatical, not encyclopedic, and a moment's reflection will show that whole areas of culture were of so little interest to eighteenth-century man in America that we can safely ignore them. One such is the middle ages; and whatever subtleties the schoolmen, including St. Thomas, lavished upon the analysis of happiness, Protestant America in the Age of Revolution was not directly affected by them.[2] Jefferson's generation, so far as it read about happiness in books, drew upon antiquity; it drew, in lesser degree, upon the

[1] L. Maxcy, Inc., *et al. v.* Mayo, 139 Sou. 121.

[2] However, see in this connection John C. Ford, S. J., "The Natural Law and the 'Pursuit of Happiness,'" *Notre Dame Lawyer,* XXVI (1951), 429 f.

Bible, upon Calvinism, and upon renaissance speculation; and it drew upon seventeenth-century thought and, of course, upon speculation in the Age of Reason. Perhaps we can catch some suggestive hints concerning happiness in at least some of these several phases of history.

ii

In his volume, *Modern Democracies,* James Bryce observed about a quarter of a century ago that American Revolutionary leaders went back two thousand years for their inspiration.[1] The remark was not then so obvious as it now sounds. An earlier generation had pictured Pilgrim, Puritan, and even Cavalier, fleeing under Providence in search of liberty and simultaneously bringing liberty with them. This mystical interpretation by and by faded into the theory of an identity of British and American Whiggism; this, in turn, into the general concept of democratic institutions sprouting wherever a branch of the Teutonic people settled; and when this theory revealed its inadequacies, there developed simultaneously a theory of economic determinism and a tendency to equate American revolutionary thought with the philosophic radicalism of eighteenth-century France. Modern scholarship tends to return us, as it were, to the observation of Bryce. Inasmuch as genteel education in America, despite the reforms of Franklin, was still, as we say, classical, it is not surprising that classical thought, usually in its more commonplace forms, should have molded the minds of the gentry who wrote, or accepted, the Virginia bill of rights and the Declaration of Independence.

In what ways is the American concept of the pursuit of happiness rooted in antiquity? I suggest two aspects of the problem. One is happiness as an ethico-political concept, and the other is happiness as a way of living. One

[1] James Bryce, *Modern Democracies* (2 vols.; New York, 1921), I, 3; 165.

affects the other; yet in general the first idea is associated with the familiar line of development from Plato through Epicurean and Stoic thought; and the other is particularly influential as expressed by Horace. If we are to understand the matter, however, we must put aside modern interpretation of the Greeks and the Romans and, contenting ourselves with commonplaces, try to look at the writers of antiquity as those elegant models of expression and conduct which the eighteenth-century gentleman theoretically sought to imitate. Chronology in this approach is of small significance.

In the Fifth Book of the *Tusculan Disputations* Cicero tries to answer the question whether virtue is sufficient for a happy life. Not unnaturally he finds that it is. But I think we can get a clearer notion of classical theories of happiness if we turn to the sympathetic explication of the nobler parts of Epicurus, in sections xvii, xviii, and xix of Cicero's *De Finibus,* an essay on the chief good and the chief evil of human life. In somewhat condensed form this is what Cicero says:

> . . . we admit that the pleasures and pains of the mind are caused by the pleasures and pains of the body. . . But although pleasure of mind brings us joy, and pain causes us grief, it is still true that each of these feelings originates in the body . . . and it does not follow on that account that both the pleasures and pains of the mind are not much more important than those of the body. For with the body we are unable to feel anything which is not actually existent and present; but with our mind we feel things past and things to come . . . the very greatest pleasure or annoyance of the mind contributes more to making life happy or miserable than either of these feelings can do if it is in the body for an equal length of time . . . as we are roused by those good things which we are in expectation of, so we rejoice at those which we recollect. But foolish men are tortured by the recollection of past evils; wise men are de-

> lighted by the memory of past good things, which are thus renewed by the agreeable recollection. But there is a feeling implanted in us by which we bury adversity as it were in a perpetual oblivion, but dwell with pleasure and delight on the recollection of good fortune. . . Oh what a splendid, and manifest, and simple, and plain way of living well! . . . that man cannot live agreeably, unless he lives honourably, justly, and wisely; and . . . if he lives wisely, honourably, and justly, it is impossible that he should not live agreeably . . . Therefore, there is no fool who is happy, and no wise man who is not . . . the wise man . . . has limited desires; he disregards death; he has a true opinion concerning the immortal Gods without any fear; he does not hesitate, if it is better for him, to depart from life. Being prepared in this manner, and armed with these principles, he is always in the enjoyment of pleasure; nor is there any period when he does not feel more pleasure than pain. For he remembers the past with gratitude, and he enjoys the present so as to notice how important and delightful the joys which it supplies are; nor does he depend on future good, but . . . waits for that and enjoys the present; and is as far removed as possible from vices . . . and when he compares the life of fools to his own he feels great pleasure.[1]

Here is a second, similar, and shorter statement of the classical theory of happiness, this time from the *Minor Dialogues* of Seneca:

> A happy life, therefore, is one which is in accordance with its own nature, and cannot be brought about unless in the first place the mind be sound and remain so without interruption, and, next, be bold and vigorous, enduring all things with most admirable courage, suited to the times in which it lives, careful of the body and its appurtenances, yet not troublesomely careful. It must also set due value upon all the things which adorn our lives, without over-

[1] *The Academic Questions, Treatise de Finibus, and Tusculan Disputations of M. T. Cicero,* trans. by C. D. Yonge (London, 1853), pp. 118-120.

> estimating any one of them, and must be able to enjoy the bounty of Fortune without becoming her slave.[1]

Epicurean and Stoic, Aristotelian and Platonist may vary in innumerable particulars, but they tend to agree that happiness is some form of virtuous activity. For Aristotle happiness is fulfillment of function; and since nothing can be truly happy except in proportion as it fulfills its function, the happiness of man must arise out of that which distinguishes him as man from the rest of creation, particularly from the brutes. This happiness, he says, "we define as the active exercise of the mind in conformity with perfect goodness or virtue."[2] Since contemplation is the highest form of activity because the intellect is the highest part of man's nature, and since we can reflect more continuously than we can do anything else, it follows that philosophic contemplation is the most pleasurable of all activities in conformity with virtue. To be sure, contemplation obviously implies leisure to contemplate; the masses, who have no leisure, are therefore misled into thinking that mere enjoyment is the end of life, but this is to degrade mankind to the level of the cattle, it is not life in accordance with the nature of things—in this case, the essence of being a man. Only the philosopher can be truly happy.

I have deliberately discussed Aristotle after the more commonplace Cicero and Seneca, because it is only when one sees the reasoning behind the commonplace that one understands the force of the idea. It is, however, evident from these three statements that classical happiness is

[1] This is from *De Vita Beata,* but I have forgotten whose translation I have employed. See, however, *Seneca: Moral Essays,* trans. by John W. Basore, in the Loeb Classical Library (3 vols.; London and New York, 1928-1935), II, 107, for an excellent version.

[2] *Aristotle's Ethics for English Readers: Rendered from the Greek of the Nicomachean Ethics,* trans. by H. Rackham (Oxford: Basil Blackwell, 1943), p. 28.

particularly the function of an aristocrat possessing both leisure and intelligence. It arises from reason, even among the Epicureans, because the perfected private judgment mirrors the order of nature and is content in that order. The enemies of this way of life are the body itself, which may mislead the mind; and also society at large, which, being built upon convention, is artificial and an obstacle to an understanding of the order of nature. Man-made law and custom are likely to be the enemies of wisdom, which is resignation to the order of the universe. Law and custom are mere local authorities which, in the nature of the case, cannot be divine. Therefore it is that ancient writers, though they cite with admiration (as Cicero does) examples of Roman virtue, such as Virginius slaying his own daughter and Brutus condemning his son to death, do not, as it were, confuse these with either patriotism or social service, the sanction of such deeds being from the universe and not from the state. To live according to nature is to be happy; that is, one does not mistake the social order for the eternal order of things.

Translate this relatively melancholy view of the universe into Christian terms not too closely defined, and you will find an acceptance of resignation to the eternal order no small part of the thinking of the founding fathers. That fiery spirit, Samuel Adams, for example, strove to reconcile himself and others to an inward sense of virtue as a compensation for sorrow and disappointment. Thus in 1772 he wrote his brother-in-law, Andrew Elton Wells, who had just lost a sister by death, that:

> We too often mistake our true Happiness, and when we arrive to the Enjoyment of that which seemed to promise it to us, we find that it is all an imaginary Dream, at the best fleeting and transitory. . . . [Yet] to be possessed of the Christian Principles, & to accommodate our whole Deportment to such Principles, is to be happy in this Life . . . and

puts it out of the power of the World to disappoint us by any of its frowns.[1]

As for himself, he wrote William Checkley that same year:

It is not an easy thing at this time of my Life, to put me out of the possession of my self. I have been used to the alternate Frowns & Smiles of many who call themselves, & some of them in truth are my Friends. I bear it all with Œquanimity, infinitely better pleas[e]d with the Approbation of my own mind, than I should be with the flatteries of the Great, & in the Sunshine of power.[2]

Seven years later he told John Adams:

While I am in this world I am resolv[e]d that no Vexation shall put me out of Temper if I can possibly command myself. Even old Age which is making Strides toward me shall not prevail to make me peevish. . . . You who are in the Midst of Life & Usefulness, do not expect to escape the envenom[e]d Shaft, but you have always the Cure at hand, Moderation, Fortitude & Prudence.[3]

These are striking enough; but for a full-length view of happiness in a disappointing world another letter to John Adams (October 4, 1790), despite the length of the passage, deserves to be quoted, for in it philosophical disillusion and philosophic calm are strangely mingled:

You ask what the World is about to become? and, Is the Millenium commencing? I have not studied the Prophesies, and cannot even conjecture. The Golden Age so finely pictured by Poets, I believe has never yet existed; but in their own imaginations. In the earliest periods, when for the honor of human nature, one should have thought, that man had not learnt to be cruel; what Scenes of horror have

[1] *Writings of Samuel Adams,* edited by H. A. Cushing (4 vols.: New York, 1904-1908), II, 337-338. See in this connection his letter of advice to Joseph Allen, November 7, 1771, II, 268 f.

[2] The same, II, 381.

[3] The same, IV, 131-132.

> been exhibited in families of some of the best instructors in Piety and morals! Even the heart of our first father was grievously wounded at the sight of the murder of one of his Sons, perpetrated by the hand of the other. Has Mankind since seen the happy Age? No, my friend. The same Tragedys have been acted on the Theatre of the World, the Arts of tormenting have been studied and practiced to this day; and true religion, and reason united have never succeeded to establish the permanent foundations of political freedom, and happiness in the most enlightened Countries on the Earth. After a compliment to Boston Town meetings, and our Harvard College as having "set the universe in Motion"; you tell me Every Thing will be pulled down; I think with you, "So much seems certain," but what say you, will be built up? Hay, wood and stubble, may probably be the materials, till Men shall be yet more enlightened, and more friendly to each other. "Are there any Principles of Political Architecture?" Undoubtedly. "What are they?" Philosophers, ancient and modern, have laid down different plans, and *all* have thought themselves, masters of the true Principles. Their Disciples have followed them, probably with a blind prejudice, which is always an Enemy to truth, and have thereby added fresh fuel to the fire of Contention, and increased the political disorder. Kings have been deposed by aspiring Nobles, whose pride could not brook restraint. These have waged everlasting War, against the common rights of Men.

To be sure, the love of liberty is inherent in the soul of man; but wars of liberation

> have too often ended in nothing more than a "change of Impostures, and impositions." The Patriots of Rome put an End to the Life of Caesar, and Rome submitted to a Race of Tyrants in his stead. Were the People of England free, after they had obliged King John to concede to them their ancient rights, and Libertys, and promise to govern them according to the Old Law of the Land? . . . while we daily see the violence of human passions controuling the Laws

> of Reason and religion, and stifling the very feelings of humanity; can we wonder, that in such tumults little or no regard is had to Political Checks and Ballances? And such tumults have always happened within as well as without doors. The best formed constitutions that have yet been contrived by the wit of Man have, and will come to an End—because "the Kingdoms of the Earth have not been governed by Reason."

Adams could find for this sorrowful state of humanity only one vague cure: education in virtue—"inculcating in the Minds of youth the fear, and Love of the Deity, and universal Phylanthropy . . . leading them in the Study, and Practice of the exalted Virtues of the Christian system." Perhaps the millennium might reveal a republican form of government, but he was not sure. Resignation and virtue were the only hope.[1]

Nor was John Adams of a differing philosophy. Though, as he said in *Thoughts on Government* (1776), the true end of government is "the happiness of society," just as the true end of man is "the happiness of the individual," his great treatise, *Discourses on Davila* (1790), matches Machiavelli's *Discourses on the First Decade of Titus Livius* in its sardonic disillusion about government and history. Simple benevolence is no counterbalance to selfishness, and the mean desire of reputation is seen to be the driving force in human nature. At the age of twenty Adams thought this world "not designed for a lasting and a happy state, but rather for a state of moral discipline"; and three years later he wrote:

> It is in vain to expect felicity without an habitual contempt of fortune, fame, beauty, praise, and all such things; unaffected benevolence to men, and conscious integrity, are sufficient supports—

[1] The same, IV, 340-343.

the classic doctrines of "*animi magnitudo* and *rerum humanarum contemptio*" which "alone secure . . . happiness."[1] Toward the end of the *Discourses on Davila* he said:

> . . . there are other causes enough, which will forever prevent perpetuity or tranquillity, in any great degree, in human affairs. Animal life is a chemical process, and is carried on by unceasing motion. Our bodies and minds, like the heavens, the earth, and the sea, like all animal, vegetable, and mineral nature, like the elements of earth, air, fire, and water, are continually changing. The mutability and mutation of matter, and much more of the intellectual and moral world, are the consequences of laws of nature, not less without our power than beyond our comprehension.[2]

Trust in equal laws and in deity was his frail and solitary philosophic hope:

> In the wisdom, power, and goodness of our maker is all the security we have against roasting in volcanoes and writhing with the tortures of gout, stone, cholic, and cancers; sinking under the burdens of dray-horses and hackney coach-horses to all eternity. Nature produces these evils, and if she does it by chance, she may assign them all to us, whether we behave well or ill, and the poor hag will not know what she does.
>
> Resignation is our own affair. What good does it do to God? Prudence dictates to us to make the best we can of inevitable evils. We may fret and fume and peeve and scold and rave, but what good does this do?[3]

It is scarcely necessary to quote extensively from Franklin, whose "The Ephemera" (1778) exactly, if good-naturedly, illustrates the vanity of human life. Yet a letter

[1] John Adams, *Works,* II, 29, 65-66.
[2] The same, VI, 394.
[3] The same, IX, 589; X, 220.

of his to Joseph Huey written as early as 1753 may conclude this chain of passages illustrating the "Christianization" of ancient philosophy in eighteenth-century America:

> For my own Part, when I am employed in serving others, I do not look upon myself as conferring Favours, but as paying Debts. In my Travels, and since my Settlement, I have received much Kindness from Men, to whom I shall never have any Opportunity of making the least direct Return. And numberless Mercies from God, who is infinitely above being benefited by our Services. Those kindnesses from Men, I can therefore only Return on their Fellow Men; and I can only shew my Gratitude for these mercies from God, by a readiness to help his other Children and my Brethren. For I do not think that Thanks and Compliments, tho' repeated weekly, can discharge our real Obligations to each other, and much less those to our Creator. You will see in this my Notion of good Works, that I am far from expecting . . . to merit Heaven by them. By Heaven we understand a State of Happiness, infinite in Degree, and eternal in Duration: I can do nothing to deserve such rewards: He that for giving a Draught of Water to a thirsty Person, should expect to be paid with a good Plantation, would be modest in his Demands, compar'd with those who think they deserve Heaven for the little good they do on Earth. Even the mix'd imperfect Pleasures we enjoy in this World, are rather from God's Goodness than our Merit: how much more such Happiness of Heaven.[1]

As he wrote "Katy" Ray two years later: "I hope . . . to bear with patience and dutiful submission any change [God] may think fit to make that is less agreeable."[2] Thus it was that the classical doctrine of happiness as resignation to the course of things was domesticated in America.

[1] *Writings,* III, 144. The whole letter, by the way, oddly anticipates the theory of the social gospel.

[2] The same, III, 282.

iii

But if leading Americans thus accepted happiness as *theoria* or the disinterested contemplation of truth, they also interested themselves in another form of felicity. The life of Horace gave them an influential example of carrying out happiness in practical living. Aristotle required a moderate furnishing of material goods in order to insure leisure for contemplation, and obviously, as other philosophers pointed out, health and strength are also desirable. All these things Horace had or sought. Cured of political ambition by the civil wars, he retreated from the hurly-burly of Rome and politics, and advised his friends to do likewise so far as they could—leave the clients in the anteroom, he says, and skip out by the back door. Maecenas gave him a modest estate on the Sabine River. It had a comfortable house—a *villula,* he calls it—standing in a little field *(agella)*. There were five tenant farmers to keep him supplied. There was a fine view. There was a spring, which never dried up; a garden, not too elaborate; vineyards, apparently yielding an adequate little wine; and woods extensive enough to feed the herd of pigs with acorns and furnish the master with shade. The temperature was neither too hot nor too cold. Here, said he, I live and rule—*vivo et regno*. Here, when his friends came, they had the famous nights and suppers of the gods. Here, in short, far from the madding crowd's ignoble strife, he lived comfortably, accepting with only a minimum of regret the changes of time.

> omnem crede diem tibi diluxisse supremum,
> grata superveniet quae non sperabitur hora.[1]

Reconciled to the eternal order, Horace spent each day as if it were going to be his last, and was every morning grateful that a peaceful morrow had dawned. Such an

[1] *Epistles,* I, iv, 13-14.

existence passed beyond mere hedonism into the eudaimonism of Aristotle, and exemplified the ideal which holds, to quote Cicero again, that "a man . . . who is temperate and consistent, free from fear or grief, and uninfluenced by any immoderate joy or desire, cannot be otherwise than happy."[1]

Classical doctrine approaches a spectator theory of felicity, a theory which had great vogue among the American upper class in the eighteenth century. Poets and men of affairs dreamed of a new Sabine farm on the banks of the Schuylkill River or the Hudson, at Poplar Grove or Braintree, Massachusetts, at Monticello or Boston. Thus in 1732, in an endeavor to console Governor Belcher for the death of his son-in-law, the Rev. Mather Byles wrote a poem to say that Daniel Oliver had been a happy man on his New England Sabine farm:

> Mindless of Grandieur, from the Crowd he fled,
> Sought green Retirements, and the silent Shade.
> Ye bow'ry Trees, which round his Mansion bloom,
> Oft ye conceal'd him in your hallow'd Gloom:
> Oft he enjoy'd, in your sublime Abode,
> His Books, his Innocence, his Friend, his GOD.
> . . . I wander O'er the lofty Seat,
> And trace the Mazes of the soft Retreat.
> View the fair Prospects, round the Gardens rove,
> Bend up the Hill, and search the lonely Grove;
> . . . .
> I seem to meet him in the flow'ry Walks,
> And, thro' the Boughs, his whispering Spirit talks. . .[2]

Again, in 1747 William Livingston published his *Philosophic Solitude; or, The Choice of a Rural Life. A Poem.*

1 *The Academic Questions,* p. 448.

2 *A Sermon . . . Occasion'd By the much Lamented Death of The Honourable Daniel Oliver, Esq.; . . . By Thomas Prince . . . With a Poem by Mr. Byles* (Boston, 1732). The quotation may be found on page 3 of Byles's poem, "An Elegy."

By a Gentleman educated at Yale College, a work which pictures the delights of a rural mansion and tranquillity, where friends, the calm contemplation of the universe, a choice library, good wine, and a New World Lalage—

> With her I'd spend the pleasurable day,
> While fleeting minutes gayly danc'd away—

sufficiently echo Horace in the royal province of New York. Imitating the British poet Pomfret, Benjamin Church in *The Choice* (Boston, 1757) poetically desired to breathe away half his life in a rural retreat with books, good wine, hospitality for a few choice friends and the needy stranger; and describes his country seat in part as follows:

> Eastward my moderate Fields should wave with Grain,
> Southward the Verdure of a broad Champaign;
> Where gamesome Flocks, and rampant Herds might play,
> To the warm Sun-shine of the Vernal Day;
> Northward, a Garden on a Slope should lye,
> Finely adjusted to the nicest Eye. . .
> Westward, I'd have a thick-set Forest grow,
> Thro' which the bounded Sight should scarcely go. . .[1]

and there, accompanied by a new Eve, "soberly serene," he planned to adore his Creator and give his mind to the contemplation of virtue. The picture was repainted by Benjamin West, of Providence, in 1765:

> A small Estate, some hundred Pounds a Year,
> From Taxes, Tithes, and such Incombrance, clear;
> A little Cottage, on a rising Ground,
> With nothing useless in it to be found:
> I'd chuse to have it front the Noon-Day's Sun,
> And not far distant from a neighb'ring Town,
> With some few Acres round it to supply
> What's just sufficient for the Family—

[1] [Benjamin Church], *The Choice: A Poem, After the Manner of Mr. Pomfret. By a young Gentleman* (Boston, 1757), pp. 10-11.

Horace's *villula* and *agella*—and there West will enjoy the charms of his Sylvia and a mind at ease.[1]

Nor was all this mere poetry. It was an ideal actively pursued. In his old age John Adams wrote Jefferson that James Harris' dialogue concerning happiness was the best discussion of the subject he had ever read;[2] and if one turns to this once celebrated author, one finds in an essay profusely supported by Greek and Latin quotations that

> The sovereign good, as constituted by rectitude of conduct, has, on our strictest scrutiny, appeared to be this: to live perpetually selecting, as far as possible, what is congruous to nature, and rejecting what is contrary.
>
> . . . behold one of the fairest and most amiable of objects; behold the true and perfect man: that ornament of humanity, that god-like being, who, without regard either to pleasure or pain, uninfluenced equally by either prosperity or adversity, superior to the world and its best and worst events, can fairly rest his all upon the rectitude of his own conduct, can constantly, and uniformly, and manfully maintain it; thinking that, and that alone, wholly sufficient to make him happy.[3]

As early as 1773 Adams conceived that his public life was over. He wrote therefore:

> In this situation I should have thought myself the happiest man in the world, if I could have retired to my little hut and forty acres, which my father left me in Braintree, and lived on potatoes and sea-weed for the rest of my life.
>
> My resolutions to devote myself to the pleasures, the studies, the business, and the duties of private life are a source of

[1] Benjamin West, *The New-England Almanack; or, Lady's and Gentleman's Diary. For the Year of Our Lord Christ, 1766* (Providence, [1765]). This almanac lacks pagination, but the poem is entitled "The Wish. By Captain *******." Even if this is stolen from British sources, the ideal was acceptable.

[2] *Works,* X, 387-388. This letter is dated January 17, 1820.

[3] *The Works of James Harris, Esq.: With an Account of His Life and Character by His Son The Earl of Malmesbury* (Oxford, 1841), pp. 83; 91.

> ease and comfort to me that I scarcely ever experienced before.

In February 1774 he bought of his brother the paternal homestead, thirty-five acres, together with eighteen acres of pasture land, and the old house:

> The buildings and the water I wanted very much; that beautiful, winding, meandering brook, which runs through the farm always delighted me.

He set to dreaming of rural improvements; and eight years after this, writing James Warren from The Hague, he said:

> Oh peace! when wilt thou permit me to visit Penns-hill, Milton-hill, and all the blue hills? I love every tree and every rock upon all those mountains. Roving among these, and the quails, partridges, squirrels, etc., that inhabit them, shall be the amusement of my declining years.

In 1784, writing Mrs. Warren from Auteuil just after his salary had been reduced by Congress, he said that court life made no man happy, that he envied her rural occupations at Neponset Hill, that he felt more disposed to whine like Cicero or Bolingbroke over his exile from Braintree, an old, blind, disappointed man, but that

> My little farm is now my only resource, and books for amusement, without much improvement or a possibility of benefiting the world by my studies.[1]

Meanwhile, eulogizing General Montgomery at Philadelphia in 1776, William Smith found it admirable in that hero that he

> chose a delightful retirement upon the banks of Hudson's river, at a distance from the noise of the busy world! . . . In this most eligible of all situations, the life of a country gentleman, deriving its most exquisite relish from reflec-

[1] *Works,* II, 312, 314, 326; IX, 512-513, 528.

tion upon past dangers, and past services, he gave full scope to his philosophic spirit, and taste for rural elegance.[1]

Franklin advised Dr. John Fothergill in 1764:

> By the way, when do you intend to live?—*i.e.,* to enjoy life. When will you retire to your villa, give yourself repose, delight in viewing the operations of nature in the vegetable creation, assist her in her works, get your ingenious friends at times about you, make them happy with your conversation, and enjoy theirs: or, if alone, amuse yourself with your books and elegant collections?

One of the things that reconciled Franklin to living in France was the Horatian quality of his villa at Passy:

> You wish to know how I live. It is in a fine House, situated in a neat Village, on high Ground, half a Mile from Paris, with a large Garden to walk in. I have abundance of Acquaintance, dine abroad Six Days in seven. Sundays I reserve to dine at home, with such Americans as pass this Way; and I then have my Grandson Ben, with some other American Children from his school.

In a letter of 1785, on the need of resignation to the world's state, he admired a song called "The Old Man's Wish" and enumerated a warm house in a country town, an easy horse, some good old authors, ingenious and cheerful companions, a pudding on Sunday, stout ale, a bottle of burgundy, and governing one's passions as the *summum bonum* of age.[2]

Often as George Washington left Mount Vernon at the call of duty, he left it with a sigh. As he wrote James Anderson in 1797:

> I am once more seated under my own Vine and fig tree, and hope to spend the remainder of my days, which in the ordi-

1 William Smith, *An Oration, in Memory of General Montgomery* (Philadelphia, 1776), pp. 12-13.

2 *Writings,* IV, 221; VII, 223; IX, 332-333.

> nary course of things (being in my Sixty sixth year) cannot be many, in peaceful retirement, making political pursuits yield to the more rational amusement of cultivating the Earth.[1]

As for Jefferson, Monticello was his Sabine farm, which to leave so grieved him that his political opponents taxed him with craftiness, though I see no reason to doubt the sincerity of the mood in which he invariably returned to his quiet plantation. Among innumerable passages in his letters I quote these characteristic sentences to Kosciusko after Jefferson had left the White House:

> I am retired to Monticello, where, in the bosom of my family, and surrounded by my books, I enjoy a repose to which I have been long a stranger. My mornings are devoted to correspondence. From breakfast to dinner, I am in my shops, my garden, or on horseback among my farms; from dinner to dark, I give to society and recreation with my neighbors and friends; and from candle light to early bed-time, I read. My health is perfect; and my strength considerably reinforced by the activity of the course I pursue. . . . I talk of ploughs and harrows, of seeding and harvesting, with my neighbors, and of politics too, if they choose, with as little reserve as the rest of my fellow citizens, and feel, at length, the blessing of being free to say and do what I please. . .[2]

This is, as it were, the Virginia version of Virgil's *Georgics*. Such was the ideal of happiness among the cultivated gentlemen of the Revolutionary generation.

iv

But the spectator theory of happiness propounded by classical writers and adapted by Americans enjoying suf-

[1] *Writings of George Washington* (Bicentennial edition, Washington) 35, 432.

[2] *The Works of Thomas Jefferson,* XII, 369. This letter is dated February 26, 1810.

ficient wealth to practice it developed rivals. In the minds of thinkers like Philo Judaeus, to live according to nature was fused with the injunction to live according to the law revealed to Moses.[1] One was not only to follow reason and virtue, he was also to love God and obey His commandments. The happiness of the philosophers was fused with the blessedness promised to the righteous. These blessings as set forth in Scripture were frequently tangible and temporal—freedom from disease, health, keenness of sense, riches, honors, the praise of the just, a quiver full of goodly children. Modified by the church fathers, this doctrine passed into the inescapable paradox of Christian theology. On the one hand, as St. Augustine taught, since life in this world of sin is a terrifying experience, the supreme good is life eternal; but on the other hand, since God created the world, it cannot be wholly evil, and, moreover, He has made certain promises to the faithful here and now. St. Thomas might declare that man's ultimate happiness consists in the contemplation of divine truth rather than in external things, which are goods of chance; but among Protestant thinkers after Calvin, this lofty mysticism did not solve the clash between the covenant of works and the covenant of grace. Ideally, moreover, one should not lay up treasures upon earth, where moth and rust corrupt and thieves break in and steal, but the Judaeo-Christian tradition had also to deal with such embarrassing statements as that in the First Psalm:

> Blessed is the man that walketh not in the counsel of the ungodly, nor standeth in the way of sinners, nor sitteth in the seat of the scornful.
>
> But his delight is in the law of the Lord; and in his law doth he meditate day and night.

[1] See the magisterial study by Harry Austryn Wolfson, *Philo; foundations of religious philosophy in Judaism, Christianity and Islam* (Cambridge, Harvard University Press, 2 vols., 1947.)

> And he shall be like a tree planted by the rivers of water, that bringeth forth his fruit in his season; his leaf also shall not wither; and whatsoever he doeth shall prosper.

This picture of prosperity is very agreeable; and theologians, notably Calvinist thinkers, set to work to rationalize it by developing the doctrine of two callings, by which, as a commentator sardonically observes, God sprinkles holy water on economic success. Let us glance at the flowering of this notion in the New World.

In 1701 the Rev. Cotton Mather published *A Christian at His Calling. Two Brief Discourses. One Directing a Christian in his General Calling; Another, Directing him in his Personal Calling,* which sums up the theory. One's calling and election to be saved were happiness, but so was one's vocation in this world. The doctrine was already old in North America. In 1656, in a work called *A Practicall Commentary,* then in its second edition, the Rev. John Cotton assured the Christian reader that

> we may desire Wealth of God, partly for our necessity, and expediency, and partly to leave to our Posterity . . .[1]

For the Rev. John Eliot, in *The Harmony of the Gospels* (1678), prosperity was easily equated with righteousness:

> Wealth is an exercise of the dominion of man, therefore it exalts a man in the World. poverty strippeth man of his dominion, therefore it layes him low in the world.[2]

Would you have the Christian inferior to the infidel? He is worse than an infidel, wrote John Winthrop earlier, that "provideth not for his owne," since it is only by accumulating wealth that we can provide occasions when the Lord

[1] John Cotton, *A Practicall Commentary, Or An Exposition with Observations, Reasons, and Uses upon the First Epistle Generall of John* (London, 1656). However, I have used a second edition (1658), in which the quoted matter appears on p. 132.

[2] John Eliot, *The Harmony of the Gospels. In The Holy History of the Humiliation and Sufferings of Jesus Christ, from His Incarnation to His Death and Burial* (Boston, 1678), p. 39.

shall call upon us.[1] The Rev. Benjamin Colman of Boston informed the Great and General Court in 1719 that God

> fits persons for the days and for the places which he allots unto them; and by differing Genius directs and inclines one to this calling and abode, and another to that. He forms one man for his husbandry and another for his merchandize. One loves the Seacoast and another the Inland; One the trading busy Town, and another the retir'd silent Villages.

But each will

> depend on the continued watch of Divine Providence, to preserve their substance from fires and from thieves, from moth and rust and vermine; And yet when they open their stores for sale, they still depend on the direction of Providence. . .[2]

The next year the Rev. Thomas Symmes enjoined the Ancient and Honourable Artillery Company of Boston to remember that God

> requires and expects, that every Man should *abide in his Calling,* and *seek to excel* in his own Sphaere, in the Improvement of all his Endowments and Enjoyments for the Honour of GOD, his Bountiful Benefactor, and the interest of his Prince and Country.[3]

Long before learned judges thought to sanction the happiness of free enterprise by an appeal to Adam Smith, Book One, chapter 10, it is clear, the accumulation of wealth by Christians as an object of happiness in this world and a surrogate of happiness in the life to come

[1] John Winthrop, *A Modell of Christian Charity,* edited by S. E. Morison, *Old South Leaflets* [IX], No. 207, pp. 9, 10.

[2] Benjamin Colman, *The Blessing of Zebulun & Issachar. A Sermon Preached before the Great and General Court or Assembly in Boston. November 19, 1719* (Boston, 1719), p. 8.

[3] Thomas Symmes, *Good Soldiers Described, and Animated. A Sermon Preached before the Honourable Artillery Company, in Boston, June 6th. 1720 . . .* (Boston, 1720), p. 2.

had received the blessing of the clergy. If gentlemen were to have leisure for virtuous retirement, they must first be given an honorable chance to acquire wealth.

The statements are individual and partitive, but you had only to secularize and generalize the idea to arrive at economic happiness as a political aim. This was particularly done in the later eighteenth century. The charitable man, said the Rev. Samuel Cooper in 1753, accepting the doctrine of vocation,

> forms Designs of enlarging the Wealth and Power of his Country, by enlarging it's Commerce . . . and by introducing and encouraging the most useful Arts and Manufactures,

inasmuch as "Mutual Benevolence" is a fundamental law of human nature.[1] Four years later the Rev. Ebenezer Pemberton painted a happy Christian commonwealth, the result of holy vocationalism:

> Every one content with his Lot, would rejoice in the Prosperity of his Neighbour.—The Great would command without Haughtiness, and the Inferiors submit without Murmuring—The Rich would employ their superfluous Wealth, to relieve the Miseries of the Poor; and the Poor gratefully acknowledge the Kindness of their Benefactors —Envy would be banished from among Equals, and Contentions finished by mutual Concessions. There would be no Infidelity in Friendship; no Censuring in Conversation. Every one by mutual good Offices [would] become useful and agreeable to each other. This People would enjoy a Tranquility which would be a bright Resemblance of that, which is possess'd by the Saints above.[2]

1 Samuel Cooper, *A Sermon Preached in Boston, New-England, before the Society for Encouraging Industry, and Employing the Poor; August 8, 1753* (Boston, 1753), pp. 1, 12.

2 Ebenezer Pemberton, *A Sermon Preached in the Audience of the Honourable His Majesty's Council, and the Honourable House of Representatives, of the Province of the Massachusetts-Bay in New-England, May 25th. 1757 . . .* (Boston, 1757), p. 15.

Or again, the very year that James Otis published his *Rights of the British Colonies Asserted and Proved,* in Boston the Rev. James Dana printed a sermon in which, after asserting that God assists men to use their capacity "or any external advantage put into their hands," and further declaring that the parable of the talents proves that

> particular persons also . . . are variously furnished for improvement in knowledge and virtue, power and riches; and in general, for being useful in the world in different relations and capacities,

he went on to say:

> We have various connections with our fellow creatures, and different relations in society; are qualified in different respects and degrees to be helpful to one another; are mutually dependent: Consequently, we are not at liberty to use or neglect our talents, or manage them as we please. The mutual wants of mankind oblige to an interchange of kind offices. He that has no desire, takes no care, to be serviceable in his place, practically disowns his relation to society, and can have no claim to be treated as a member of it. . . If we are not the original proprietors of our respective advantages and opportunities; if they are trusts committed to us by the all-wise creator and governor of the universe, then we are indispensably bound to improve them in his service. . .[1]

We have almost got to the plain common sense of the matter.

V

But the spectator theory of happiness for the aristocrat and the prosperity theory for the Christian merchant have

[1] James Dana, *The Character and Reward of the Good and Faithful Servant. A Sermon Occasioned by the Much Lamented Death of Charles Whittlesey, Esq. . . .* (Boston, 1764), pp. 4, 18.

only an indirect or negative relation to the idea of happiness as the aim of civil society. How pass from individual happiness to the doctrine that the pursuit of happiness has something to do with government? Much learning has been expended on the antecedents of Jefferson's famous phrase. The words or something like them have been found in Locke, in Wollaston, in Adam Smith, in Bolingbroke, in Frances Hutcheson, in Hume, in Lord Kames, in Blackstone, in Burlamaqui, in Hobbes, in Beccaria, in John Hall, even in Oliver Goldsmith and Dr. Johnson. Jefferson himself has been labeled a stoic, an epicurean, a deist, a utilitarian, a materialist, a romantic, a disciple of French thought, a classicist, and a follower of Jesus as the search has gone forward. The results of inquiry have been interesting, but they have also been kaleidoscopic.

Thus, for Professor Ralph Henry Gabriel, American constitutional theory, including the doctrine of rights, parallels the cosmic constitutionalism of the Newtonian era; and the foundation of our democratic faith is found, he thinks, in a frank supernaturalism deriving from Christianity.[1] For Professor Roland Bainton, however, the emphasis is elsewhere; he thinks the appalling vastness of the Copernican universe drove government beyond theology and made the finality of sheer individualism the basis of the rights of man.[2] But Professor Herbert D. Foster derives American theory from international Calvinism by way of Locke, Blackstone, and other worthies.[3] Professor R. M. MacIver, however, though he grants that the Americans hunted down precedents for doing what they would have done anyway, can find no speculative

[1] Ralph Henry Gabriel, "Constitutional Democracy: A Nineteenth-Century Faith," in Read, pp. 247-258.

[2] Roland Bainton, "The Appeal to Reason and the American Constitution," also in Read, pp. 121-130.

[3] Herbert D. Foster, "International Calvinism through Locke and the Revolution of 1688," *American Historical Review,* XXXII (April 1927), 475-499.

preparation for revolutionary theory, for the reason that by the 1770's an older American tradition had decayed.[1] Professor Ralph Barton Perry can scarcely agree. He derives the pursuit of happiness as a government aim, paradoxically enough, from Christian pessimism, which he weds to Adam Smith, thus providing, he thinks, "the standard form of reconciliation between the professed benevolence of the democratic man and the acknowledged selfishness of the economic man."[2] Who shall decide when distinguished doctors disagree?

Whatever the sources of Jefferson's statement, it seems clear that ideas cannot flourish except in a favorable climate of opinion. I suggest that one of the chief links between private happiness and the theory that the pursuit of happiness is a social aim grows out of an emotional response to the picture of North America as a land without monopolists, "engrossers," medieval restrictions, autocratic government, or theological misrule.

For, by the third quarter of the eighteenth century, it was universally understood that the New World, at least the British New World, was a happy, happy land, a model territory under a model government. Thus *The Independent Reflector,* a New York weekly, pictured the colonies in 1752:

> Under the mild and gentle Administration of a *limited* Prince, every Thing looks chearful and happy, smiling and serene. Agriculture is encouraged, and proves the annual Source of immense Riches. . . The Earth opens her fertile

1 R. M. MacIver, "European Doctrines and the Constitution," in Read, pp. 51-61.

2 Ralph Barton Perry, *Puritanism and Democracy* (New York: The Vanguard Press, 1944), p. 158. But see the whole volume. Other representative discussions include Edward Dumbauld, *The Declaration of Independence and What It Means Today* (1950); Julian P. Boyd, *The Declaration of Independence* (1945); Herbert Lawrence Ganter, "Jefferson's 'Pursuit of Happiness' and some Forgotten Men," *William and Mary Quarterly,* 2nd. series, XVI, 422 f., 558 f.

> Bosom to the Plough-share, and luxuriant Harvests diffuse Wealth and Plenty thro' the Land: The Fields stand thick with Corn: The Pastures smile with Herbage: The Hills and vallies are cover'd with Flocks and Herds: Manufacturies flourish; and unprecarious Plenty recompenses the Artificer's Toil.[1]

Is the picture too generalized? Here are two Massachusetts sermons preached at the end of the Seven Years War. Said the Rev. East Apthorp in Cambridge on August 11, 1763, discussing "The Felicity of the Times:"

> It is . . . the peculiar happiness of OUR country, that it is capable . . . of perpetual improvements, without endangering its safety by the effects of its own opulence. It will for ages admit of vast numbers of settlers from all the protestant countries of Europe; to cultivate in security our fertile lands, to enrich themselves by arts and industry, and to enjoy the freedom of our government and purity of Religion. Our climate naturally produces hardy bodies and active minds. While the slavish African and the effeminate Asiatic bow beneath the yoke of savage tyranny; Liberty and Reason make fair amends for the inclemencies of our less genial sky. Our Country will always find a sufficient employment for its inhabitants, in *agriculture* and a *simple commerce;* a circumstance, which in the natural course of things, will retard the corruption of manners and depravation of Religion. . .[2]

During the previous May, in a Boston election sermon, the Rev. Thomas Barnard had declared:

> Now commences the Æra of our Quiet Enjoyment of those Liberties, which our Fathers purchased with the Toil of their whole Lives . . . Safe from the Enemy of the Wilder-

[1] *The Independent Reflector,* December 21, 1752, p. 15.

[2] East Apthorp, *The Felicity of the Times. A Sermon Preached at Christ-Church, Cambridge, on Thursday, XI August, MDCCLXIII . . .* (Boston, 1763), p. 9.

ness, safe from the griping Hand of arbitrary Sway and cruel Superstition; Here shall be found the late founded Seat of Peace and Freedom . . . Here shall be a perennial Source of her Strength and Riches. Here shall Arts and Sciences, the Companions of Tranquillity, flourish . . . Here shall dwell uncorrupted Faith, the pure worship of God in its primitive Simplicity. . .[1]

Four Dissertations by William Smith and others was published simultaneously in London and Philadelphia in 1766; in it you will find this picture of America:

> Where ignorance and barbarity frowned over the uncultivated earth, gay fields now smile, bedecked in the yellow robe of full-eared harvest; cities rise majestic to the view; fleets too croud the capacious harbour with their swelling canvas, and swarms of chearful inhabitants cover the shore with monuments of their industry, through a long tract of two thousand miles.[2]

By 1774 this has become:

> Our fields, through the wonted providence of the great Lord of the soil, produce their usual crops—our barns expand with the pressing load of unnumbered sheaves; and a joy 'like unto the joy of harvest' spreads a serenity of countenance through thousands, ten thousand families—in pleasing confidence, and with unwearied diligence, they beat the golden ears, and prepare the joyful produce of a twelve month's labour—Whistling as they go, and forming a general concussion of earth, from every distant frontier, they roll along in *heavy loads* the grateful tribute of their toils.[3]

1 Thomas Barnard, *A Sermon Preached before his Excellency Francis Bernard, Esq. . . . May 25th. 1763* (Boston, 1763), p. 44.

2 *Four Dissertations, On the Reciprocal Advantages of a Perpetual Union between Great-Britain and her American Colonies. Written for Mr. Sargent's Prize-Medal . . .* (Philadelphia and London, 1766), p. 6.

3 [Richard Wells,] *A Few Political Reflections Submitted to the Consideration of the British Colonies by a Citizen of Philadelphia* (Philadelphia, 1774), p. 23.

Franklin, as we have seen, accepted most of the eighteenth-century notions of happiness, however contradictory they may have been. Perhaps nothing more illuminates the notion that a happy land was an agrarian land than Franklin's continuing insistence on what was for him an obvious truism. In *The Interest of Great Britain Considered with regard to Her Colonies* (1760) he had remarked:

> Manufactures are founded in poverty. It is the multitude of poor without land in a country, and who must work for others at low wages or starve, that enables undertakers to carry on a manufacture, and afford it cheap enough to prevent the importation of the same kind from abroad, and to bear the expence of its own exportation.

> But, no man who can have a piece of land of his own, sufficient by his labour to subsist his family in plenty, is poor enough to be a manufacturer [i.e., factory worker], and work for a master. Hence, while there is land enough in *America* for our people, there can never be manufactures to any amount or value.[1]

He wished that the vogue of DuPont de Nemours' agrarian *Physiocratie* might increase "till it becomes the governing philosophy of the human species;" and he advised C. W. F. Dumas, if he emigrated to America, to buy land and stock "a very good Plantation" in one of the colonies

> where the Climate is healthy, and the Government mild and good, and where if anywhere, Competence and Happiness are within the Reach of every honest, prudent & industrious Man.[2]

He contrasted the happiness of New England freeholders

[1] *Writings,* IV, 49.
[2] The same, V, 156; 152.

with the poverty of England and Scotland;[1] and, in congratulating Sir Joseph Banks on the peace, pondered on the lost opportunities for agrarian happiness:

> What vast additions to the Conveniences and Comforts of Living might Mankind have acquired, if the Money spent in Wars had been employed in Works of public utility! What an extension of Agriculture, even to the Tops of our Mountains; what Rivers rendered navigable or joined by Canals: what Bridges, Aqueducts, new Roads, and other public Works, Edifices, and Improvements. . .[2]

Even so, however, America was a truly happy land:

> The almost general mediocrity of Fortune that prevails in America obliging its People to follow some Business for subsistence, those Vices, that usually arise from Idleness, are in a great measure prevented. Industry and constant Employment are great preservatives of the Morals and Virtue of a Nation. Hence bad Examples to Youth are more rare in America, which must be a comfortable Consideration to Parents. To this may be truly added, that serious Religion under its various Denominations is not only tolerated, but respected and practised. Atheism is unknown there; Infidelity rare and secret; so that persons may live to a great Age in that Country, without having their Piety shocked by meeting with either an Atheist or an Infidel. And the Divine Being seems to have manifested his Approbation of the mutual Forbearance and Kindness with which the different Sects treat each other, by the remarkable Prosperity with which He has been pleased to favour the whole Country.[3]

1 The same, V, 362. Compare also the famous passage on the three ways of acquiring wealth: war, which is robbery; commerce, which is cheating; agriculture, "the only *honest way,* wherein man receives a real increase of the seed thrown into the ground, in a kind of continual miracle, wrought by the hand of God in his favour, as a reward for his innocent life and his virtuous industry" (V, 202).

2 The same, VIII, 593.

3 "Information to Those Who Would Remove to America" (1782), *Writings,* VIII, 613-614.

Happy, happy country, almost justifying the later decisions of American courts concerning the curse laid on Adam, the patrimony of the poor, freedom of contract, and the right to follow the vocation of one's choice! If the wretched British sought deliberately to smash this agrarian idyll by closing American ports, it merely showed how little they understood government. In one sense it is scarcely necessary to look for the philosophic antecedents of the right to happiness. The right to pursue happiness in America had, as it were, grown up in a fit of absence of mind; but if you doubted the validity of the idea, you had merely to look at the happiness around you to infer that any government which would destroy such felicity was unrighteous. *Post hoc ergo propter hoc* was as good as *quod est demonstrandum* in 1776. Such was the plain common sense of the matter.

But let us pass beyond the common sense of the matter into philosophy. The transformation of happiness into a political concept was easy and natural in the later eighteenth century. The word acquired status in the vocabulary of the genteel, a fact strongly to be inferred from the dictionaries which in that more hieratic society were principally sold to the nobility, the gentry, and the merchants. Although happiness appears in the language at least as early as 1530, an examination of thirty-one dictionaries printed between 1670 and 1797 reveals that out of fourteen compilations published before 1760,[1] only three include happiness, virtually without explication, whereas Marchant in 1760 and Johnson a few years earlier for the first time print philosophical definitions of the noun;[2] definitions which thereafter become regularly part of the furniture of these compilations. Because the

[1] I count as two the editions of Johnson in 1755 and in 1755-56. But Johnson, of course, repeats his definition.

[2] Johnson's first definition is virtually identical with his latest one, albeit the examples, or rather their titles, mildly differ in later editions.

diffused deism of the Revolutionary era was compatible both with classical culture and with sensational psychology, readers of the *Essay Concerning Human Understanding,* particularly students of Chapter XXI, "Of Power," found it easy to fuse the pleasure-pain principle of the ancients with the Lockeian doctrine of "uneasiness" which determines will, therefore desire, and therefore happiness Wrote Locke:

> Let a man be ever so well persuaded of the advantages of virtue, that it is as necessary to a man who has any great aims in this world, or hopes in the next, as food to life; yet, till he hungers or thirsts after righteousness, till he *feels an uneasiness* in the want of it, his *will* will not be determined to any action in pursuit of this professed greater good. . .[1]

The removal of this uneasiness is the first step to happiness, but the rightness of good and evil, that is, of pleasure and pain, lies in reflective comparisons. The pleasure of sensuality and the pleasure of knowledge both exist; the shortsighted rest content in the senses, but "the highest perfection of intellectual nature lies in a careful and constant pursuit of true and solid happiness";[2] and for Locke, at least in later editions of the *Essay,* true and solid happiness was found in Christianity and in society, the principle of which is justice.

There is, however, another interesting aspect of the Lockeian theory, ingeniously worked out by Professor Edmond N. Cahn, which links Locke, Jefferson, Madison, and (as we shall see) William James in a single philosophic chain.[3] Reasoning backward from the writings of James

[1] John Locke, *An Essay Concerning Human Understanding,* edited by Alexander Campbell Fraser (2 vols.; Oxford, 1894), I, 335 (Book II, chap. xxi, sec. 35).

[2] The same, I, 348 (Book II, chap. xxi, sec. 52).

[3] Edmond N. Cahn, "Madison and the Pursuit of Happiness," *New York University Law Review,* XXVII (April 1952), 265-276.

Madison, Professor Cahn holds that Madison's political philosophy corresponds to the ethical doctrines and convictions bound up in the phrase, the pursuit of happiness. Let us, he said, re-examine Locke. The supposed differentiation between property and happiness does not really exist. For Locke property is more than material possessions, it is "lives, liberties and estates," it is "that property which men have in their persons as well as goods." Property is what belongs to a man as man, not merely his physical possessions but also that extension of intangible values—life, freedom, one's stake in society—which William James was later to include in his definition of the self. And though Professor Cahn does not put the matter this way, Locke's true meaning, to which either "property" or "happiness" might in this context indifferently apply, points forward to the doctrine of self-development that is to characterize the twentieth century interpretation of happiness.

Without entering upon Professor Cahn's fascinating parallel between Madison's national republic and Locke's "individual inner republic," it will here suffice to note what this able paper has to say concerning Locke's philosophy of happiness (and therefore Jefferson's in the Declaration). Professor Cahn begins by noting that Locke completely re-wrote the chapter on power, and that "it is the later wisdom, the revised analysis" that here concerns us. What moves human desire in Locke's philosophy? Happiness, and happiness alone. Our freedom as human beings consists in our power to suspend the satisfaction of desires so that we may consider the objects we desire. When we have judged, then and then only we have done our duty, all that we can do or ought to do in the pursuit of our happiness. "As therefore," writes Locke, "the highest perfection of intellectual nature lies in a careful and constant pursuit of true and solid happiness, so the care of ourselves that we mistake not imaginary for real happiness is the necessary foundation of our liberty." But though all men seek happiness, they do not all seek the same sort of happiness. Men, he argues, may choose different things, and yet all may choose aright. "Variety and self-determination in what men pursue as their happiness is a dominant motif of Locke's doctrine."

Professor Cahn now transfers this analysis from the ethical sphere into the political sphere, and in so doing throws more light on the concept of the meaning of Jefferson's phrase than does any writer before his time. Here is the paragraph:

> These passages in Locke gave the Revolutionary period three basic philosophic notions and three corresponding ethical ideals. The first philosophic notion is that our wills are at least partly determined and impelled by non-rational factors. From this Locke inferred the ethical ideal of intellectual modesty: if reason is no absolute sovereign it cannot expect men to stand in ranks like stiff lead soldiers with painted smiles. The second philosophic notion is that our desires—short-term and long-term, lofty and earthy—compete eternally with one another in an unremitting contentiousness. The corresponding ethical ideal is diversity and variety in the individual's right to pursue his happiness. The third philosophic notion is that we have the power to suspend the execution of our desires and to exercise discriminating judgment as among them. The ethical principle based on this notion is that in their pursuit of happiness men must undertake moral responsibility for their choices. These philosophic concepts and these ethical ideals can be epitomized in the words that Jefferson selected for his Declaration. They depict the human wayfarer as he presses forward in a hopeful but everlastingly precarious pursuit. They describe the political forces in what he may justly call his "inner republic."

Madison, says this able writer, saw the basic problem of a free society in the need of paralleling in the national republic this inner republic of Locke.

But if one remains unpersuaded by Professor Cahn's acute analysis and, unsatisfied, still wonders how one passes from the individual pursuit of true and solid happiness to the assumption that the end of political society is to promote the individual happiness of its members, we find one solid bridge, at any rate, in that other great idol of eighteenth-century thinkers, Sir William Blackstone, the popularity of whose work among the Americans drew the admiration of Burke and the reproof of Jefferson. I have just said that for Locke the essence of the matter, the kernel, as it were, of liberty, is that the will is free; that is, men may choose their varying roads to happiness. Read now in the introduction to Blackstone's *Commentaries on the Laws of England,* first published from 1765 to 1769:

> [The Creator] has so intimately connected, so inseparably interwoven the laws of eternal justice with the happiness of each individual, that the latter cannot be attained but by observing the former; and, if the former be punctually obeyed, it cannot but induce the latter. In consequence of which mutual connexion of justice and human felicity, he has not perplexed the laws of nature with a multitude of abstracted rules and precepts, referring merely to the fitness or unfitness of things, as some have vainly surmised, but has graciously reduced the rule of obedience to this one paternal precept, "that man should pursue his own happiness." This is the foundation of what we call ethics, or natural law. For the several articles into which it is branched in our systems, amount to no more than demonstrating that this or that action tends to man's real happiness, and therefore very justly concluding that the performance of it is a part of the law of nature; or, on the other hand, that this or that action is destructive of man's real happiness, and therefore that the law of nature forbids it.

> This law of nature, being co-eval with mankind and dictated by God himself, is of course superior in obligation to any other. It is binding over all the globe, in all countries, and at all times: no human laws are of any validity, if contrary to this; and such of them as are valid derive all their force, and all their authority, mediately or immediately, from this original.[1]

And as Blackstone had not the slightest doubt that the aim of society is to protect individuals in the enjoyment of absolute rights springing from the law of nature and not to be preserved except by association in society, the inference is irresistible, even on his conservative premises, that

> whenever any form of Government becomes destructive of those ends, it is the Right of the People to alter or abolish it, and to institute a new Government, laying its foundations on such principles, and organizing its powers in such form, as to them shall seem most likely to effect their Safety and Happiness.

This famous passage from the Declaration of Independence brings us back by a long circuit in time to the year 1776 and the common sense of the matter, well phrased by another conservative, John Adams, in the following language:

> Upon this point all speculative politicians will agree, that the happiness of society is the end of government, as all divines and moral philosophers will agree that the happiness of the individual is the end of man. From this principle it will follow that the form of government which communicates ease, comfort, security, or, in one word, happiness, to the greatest number of persons, and in the greatest degree, is the best.[2]

[1] William Blackstone, *Commentaries on the Laws of England* (4 vols.; Oxford, 1765-1769), I, 40-41.

[2] *Works,* IV, 193. From *Thoughts on Government.*

The only difficulty in this admirable sentiment is to determine whether the greatest happiness of the population is gained by insuring the private (and contradictory) happiness of individuals or by subordinating the individual's pursuit of happiness to some larger social aim. The nineteenth century was to struggle with this problem.

IV

No Laughing Matter

IN ASSERTING THE RIGHT to pursue happiness or to pursue and obtain happiness and safety, the eighteenth-century men asserted an absolute they failed to define. This failure was natural. One's picture is that of a group of high-minded gentlemen exasperated beyond endurance and generously proclaiming principles which made resistance to tyrants obedience to God. For them the common sense of the matter was sufficient, and that which is sufficient requires neither casuistry nor metaphysics to defend it.

But what seemed self-evident in the Age of Reason sometimes becomes ambiguous in the Age of Anxiety, and as we turn to a study of certain nineteenth-century concepts of happiness, we note the development of ambiguities, partly a product of language and partly a product of logic. In the French Revolution, for instance, the rights we have been discussing became known as the Rights of Man, "man" being used generically of the species, so that Anacharsis Cloots could with consistency present himself to the French Assembly as the delegate of the human race. The language of the Declaration of Independence is not quite so clear. We read that all men are created equal and endowed with certain unalienable rights. But how is "men" to be understood? Is it equivalent to the whole human race? Or to that portion of it subscribing to the Declaration? Or is it to be taken privately, individually, and distributively? Does the sentence assert a social order, or does it mean that, whatever the social order, each individual has an unalienable right to pursue his own happiness? And is "men" meant to refer to adult males, as many court decisions seem to imply, or does it transcend sex, age, mental condition, and moral status?

The problem is not merely verbal. If what is asserted is the right of the individual to pursue happiness in his private capacity, government may become *pro tanto* the enemy of private happiness, and the courts are in duty bound to protect the individual against the leviathan state. This, in fact, some courts have done. But if the general happiness of the race is in question or, more specifically, that portion of the race organized as the United States of America, happiness as a general aim may be paramount to the anarchic pursuit of happiness by individuals, and the state may consistently demand the sacrifice of private interest for a larger social felicity. Some decisions follow this line of reasoning, which, of course, receives indirect support both from the statement in many state constitutions that the happiness of the people is the aim of government and from the general welfare provision of the federal constitution. Since, as I have earlier observed, it is difficult to make anybody happy against his will, the idea of happiness is significantly altered by this hypothesis, and the concept of natural right shifts from what was private, unalienable, and individual to what is relative, social, and public. By this interpretation what was a moral absolute arising in the nature of things is transmogrified into a legal theory governing political society and being governed by it.

The implied conflict is, in fact, upon us. For example, social security legislation may indeed make for social happiness in the long run, but it does not make for the immediate happiness of elderly businessmen who want no traffic with the welfare state. Other unalienable rights have undergone similar transformations. To contrast Leatherstocking's rifle with the inability of the sovereign people to find out anything about the atomic bomb shows what extraordinary gyrations the right to bear arms has experienced; and the transformation of the right to free speech by recent and contemporary legislation—the Revolutionary leaders, obviously conspiring to overthrow government by force and violence, would have been jailed under existing laws—parallels and illuminates what has happened to the right of pursuing happiness during the development of an agrarian culture into a gigantic industrial society.

This transformation, however, has been slow, partly because it was the product of a sluggish philosophic change as well. The eighteenth century had sought to legislate for an ideal society resting upon the unequivocal acceptance by a restricted group of citizens of a theory of natural rights as clear and evident to the gentry and the merchants as were the propositions of Euclid. The impress of these ideas did not die out in 1800. At first no one, not even Tom Paine, doubted that the physical order corresponded to the moral order, though disputes arose concerning the nature of both. In the year of Waterloo, which is, so to speak, an essentially nineteenth-century event, the aging Philip Freneau could write that

> All that we see, about, abroad,
> What is it all, but nature's God?
> In meaner works discover'd here
> No less than in the starry sphere.
> . . . .
> His system fix'd on general laws
> Bespeaks a wise creating cause;
> Impartially he rules mankind
> And all that on this globe we find.[1]

A system fixed on general laws might be either deistic or Christian, but either way it was a home for general moral truths. Even in so pessimistic a poem as "Thanatopsis"

[1] From "On the Universality and Other Attributes of the God of Nature." See *Poems of Freneau,* edited by Harry Hayden Clark, American Authors Series (New York: American Book Co., 1929), p. 422.

young Bryant interpreted stern nature as teaching lessons in axiomatic morality—man is advised to die, sustained and soothed by the same unfaltering trust which in another poem by Bryant that year guided the water-fowl from zone to zone. This was in 1817, and it is well to remember that the world had to wait almost a century for Thomas Hardy to hint that the Napoleonic wars illustrated the imbecility of the human will and the blindness of chance so dark as to suggest the unintelligent writhings of a vast amoeba.

Though the age of Wordsworth eventually replaced the Newtonian world machine by the dynamism of universal spirit, the universe of Humboldt, like the universe of Franklin, was, on the whole, intelligible in terms of general axioms. Adam Smith and Jeremy Bentham, the Scottish school of philosophy and the providential school of historians, the theology of Paley and the cosmogony of Chalmers' *Astronomical Discourses* continued to dominate an intellectual order which understood the language of the Declaration as we cannot. Culture remained rational, not anthropological. For example, the appeal of John C. Calhoun in his *A Disquisition on Government* is an appeal remote from the legal philosophy of Mr. Justice Holmes and close to fundamental law as expressed by Blackstone and understood by Jefferson. No student of such characteristic nineteenth-century magazines as *The Christian Examiner* and *The North American Review* needs to be reminded that the assertion of generalities, the appeal to deity, the assumption that the universe is both rational and benevolent, the belief that law, government, economics, morals, psychology, and therefore human nature and history can be reduced to a few sweeping principles, did not die out in the age of Jackson. Consider, indeed, this paragraph from a state paper delivered only thirty-nine years before the nineteenth century closed:

> By the frame of government under which we live, this same people have wisely given their public servants but little power for mischief; and have, with equal wisdom, provided for the return of that little to their own hands at very short intervals. While the people retain their virtue and vigilance, no administration, by any extreme of wickedness or folly, can very seriously injure the government in the short space of four years.[1]

Even a practiced ear can mistake this passage, with its talk of "frame of government," "virtue," "vigilance," "power," and "mischief" for a quotation from Jefferson, although as a matter of fact it was spoken at the national capitol on March 4, 1861, by Abraham Lincoln, almost four score and seven years after the writing of the Declaration.

Nevertheless, as the nineteenth century developed, terms like "virtue," "the pursuit of happiness," "the rights of man," and "the law of nature" tended to disappear from political discussion, or like the word "commerce," radically but quietly altered their meanings as a slow revolution in constitutional theory developed. If, in the post-Civil War period, laissez-faire economics remained the official creed of business, if at institutions like Princeton the Scottish philosophy and the faculty psychology long continued, elsewhere and in other fields the theory of animated nature melted into a doctrine of evolution red in tooth and claw; the benevolence of deity retreated into animism, pantheism, the social gospel, or a tendency not ourselves which makes for righteousness; the moral law within no longer mirrored the starry heavens without; and dogmatic theology paled its ineffectual fires in the face of folklore, comparative mythology, and the higher criticism. Young men ceased to read Blackstone as the case system took over the

[1] *The Writings of Abraham Lincoln,* edited by Arthur Brooks Lapsley (Federal ed.; 8 vols.; New York and London, 1905-1906), V, 265. The passage is from the First Inaugural Address.

law schools; young scientists ceased to aspire to chairs in natural philosophy and turned into technologists; young psychologists impatiently demanded laboratory facilities and a permanent divorce from metaphysics. The new science of sociology and the new departments of political science smiled condescendingly at the compact theory; a fourth dimension of government appeared in the invention of federal commissions to do all sorts of things that would have horrified Jefferson; and happiness ceased to have supernatural sanctions and turned into something called "adjustment" as the social worker and eventually the psychiatrist replaced the minister as a guide of life.

It is impossible in brief compass to map the path of change, but by stationing ourselves at strategic points we may acquire some notion of nineteenth-century fluctuations in the concept of felicity. For this purpose I have selected the writings of three authors sufficiently apart in time and interests, yet sufficiently outstanding as observers of American life. These are James Fenimore Cooper, Ralph Waldo Emerson, and William James. In a general sense the novelist reports on the first part of the century, the essayist on the middle years, and the philosopher helps to shape its close. The choice of Emerson and of William James is obvious; but to those for whom Cooper is still merely the author of boys' books, let me say that in succession to Franklin and Jefferson, he is par excellence the American writer to achieve international repute as an interpreter of his country and that, as Professor Herbert Schneider observes, his work is worth far more attention than it gets.[1] Cooper chronicled in novel and prose discourse the transition from the classic republic of Jefferson to the populist democracy of Jackson; he tried to reconcile the gentle-

[1] Herbert W. Schneider, *A History of American Philosophy* (New York: Columbia University Press, 1946), p. 116. See also my study of Cooper, *Tulane University Studies in English*, Vol. III, 1952.

manly virtues with the crudity of the gospel of getting on; he recorded better than any of his contemporaries the first stage in the transition from the world of George Washington to the Great Barbecue of the Robber Barons.

ii

At the beginning of our analysis of Cooper let me recall three leading components of the eighteenth-century doctrine of happiness. The first is the hypothesis that, on American equivalents of the Sabine farm, gentlemen might find philosophic happiness in a life sufficiently remote from the vulgar, yet at decent and dutiful intervals returning to public life at their country's call. The second is the theory that the virtuous Christian by following both his religious and his commercial (or other) vocation, must become prosperous and happy, since to become both is promised to the righteous. The third, cogently phrased by Blackstone, is that the law of nature being itself the product of divine benevolence, must be the only model for human law, so that in proportion as human law mirrors universal reason, citizens obedient to its ancient sanctions must secure felicity. All three of these ideas profoundly interested James Fenimore Cooper.

The writings of this great novelist are haunted by a memory and a dream. The dream is that of his father, Judge William Cooper, a democrat in emotion, a federalist by conviction, hard-headed yet philanthropic, the only landed proprietor in upper New York to escape financial ruin, who proudly declared he had settled more Americans on wilderness land than any other man in the country, and who was murdered by a political opponent. The dream is also the projection of James Fenimore Cooper as gentleman proprietor in succession; benevolent, righteous, and influential, learned in law and religion, shaping a new society into republican forms, a Roman of the best quality, guiding the lives of his clients—yeoman farmers and merchants—in a village economy, and joining other gentlemen in governing the commonwealth.

Fifteen of the thirty-one novels depend for their significance wholly or in part upon the creation, possession, management, inheritance, or loss of landed property. Real estate is of least consequence in *Lionel Lincoln,* albeit the hero goes back to practice philosophy and enjoy happiness on his English lands. In *The Spy* and *The Pilot* the ambiguous position of Mr. Wharton in the one novel and of Colonel Howard in the other is explicable by the possession of estates threatened by the rabble. In *Afloat and Ashore* and *Miles Wallingford* a dream of happiness at Clawbonny in New York—a family estate managed on Episcopalian principles—brings the hero home from the sea. He writes:

> Clawbonny never looked more beautiful than when I first cast eyes on it that afternoon. There lay the house in the secure retirement of its smiling vale, the orchards just beginning to lose their blossoms; the broad, rich meadows, with the grass waving in the south wind, resembling velvet; the fields of corn [grain] of all sorts; and the cattle, as they stood ruminating or enjoying their existence in motionless self-indulgence beneath the shade of trees, seemed to speak of abundance and considerate treatment. Everything denoted peace, plenty, and happiness.[1]

In *The Wept of Wish-ton-Wish* and in *Wyandotté* estates are lost by false religious principles; in *The Two Admirals* an estate is almost lost by a false legal principle and is regained by a true one; and in the anti-rent trilogy (*Satanstoe, The Chainbearer,* and *The Redskins*) estates are threatened by false religion, democracy, and unreasonable laws. *The Pioneers* pictures an estate in its earlier

[1] *Afloat and Ashore: A Sea Tale,* pp. 105-106. For Cooper's novels see the Leather-Stocking edition, New York, n. d., 32 volumes. The text of no American author is more carelessly reproduced.

phase of development, and in *Homeward Bound* and *Home as Found* we study the situation of its owners in the age of Jackson. Finally, the career of Mark Woolston in *The Crater* gives us the whole history of estate-making from initial discovery to its loss to demagoguery through false religion and unrighteous laws. In an avenging conclusion God sinks the land once more beneath the sea.

All this is something more than either fantasy or family pride, Cooper declares. In *Notions of the Americans* (1828), for example, he describes the home of Chief Justice John Jay, who lives on a Sabine farm. The house is less than an English country house or a French chateau, but it has the comfort of the one and some of the luxuries of the other—Horace's *villula,* in short.

> There is a mixture of use and appearance in the disposition of the grounds, that I am inclined to think very common about the residences of gentlemen of this country. The farm buildings, &c., though a little removed, were in plain view, as if their proprietor, while he was willing to escape from the inconveniences of a closer proximity, found a pleasure in keeping them at all times under his immediate eye.[1]

An adequate but unostentatious staff of servants kept up "the respectable comfort" of the establishment. As for city men, there was, up to the Jacksonian revolution, a mercantile elite in, for example, New York City, composed of men "of great leisure and large fortunes, who had imparted to their children what they had received from their fathers"[2]—note the sacrosanct character of inheritance—and who were often indistinguishable from English gentlemen.

In such establishments happiness arose from domesticity and from the fulfillment of status. Home, says Alice to John

[1] *Notions of the Americans Picked up by a Travelling Bachelor* (2 vols.; Philadelphia, 1828) I, 85.

[2] The same, I, 164.

Paul Jones in *The Pilot,* "is the dearest of all terms to every woman," and if American women should prove "ignorant of its charm, all the favors which God has lavished on their land will avail their happiness but little."[1] In contrast to European passions, says Cooper in *The Heidenmauer,* happiness in America is found "in the honest relations of the domestic circle."[2] A lady exists mainly to shed happiness upon the home, an ideal so vague as to be faintly ridiculous, yet in *Home as Found* Mr. Effingham is praised for hiring a housekeeper and freeing his daughter Eve "from cares that necessarily formed no . . . part of her duties." What her duties were does not appear, though we are told that

> to this simple and just expedient Eve was indebted for being at the head of one of the quietest, most truly elegant, and best ordered establishments in America, with no other demands on her time than that which was necessary to issue a few orders in the morning, and to examine a few accounts once a week.[3]

In *The Chainbearer* Mordaunt Littlepage hesitates to marry Ursula Malbone because she has worked for pay, but he is solaced when he learns that she was paid only half as much as a man, so that she has not violated the canons of propriety, and this leads Mordaunt (or Cooper) to declare:

> The wife of an educated man should be an educated woman; one fit to be his associate, qualified to mingle her tastes with his own, to exchange ideas, and otherwise to be his companion, in an intellectual sense. These are the higher requisites; a gentleman accepting the minor qualification as so many extra advantages, if kept within their proper limits . . . it is seldom indeed that a woman of the proper qualities may not be prevented from sinking to the level of a menial.[4]

[1] *The Pilot: A Tale of the Sea,* p. 376.
[2] *The Heidenmauer: or, The Benedictines,* p. 45.
[3] *Home as Found,* p. 2.
[4] *The Chainbearer; or, The Littlepage Manuscripts,* p. 196.

The principle of status is providential and must not be violated—the colonel's lady and Judy O'Grady are to be kept eternally apart, so much apart that Cooper can, without recognizing the absurdity, reward Lowiny Thousandacres, who, for the love of Mordaunt, has risked punishment, betrayed her family, and allowed him to escape to marry Ursula, by making her a servant in the Mordaunt household.

Status is, then, God-given and extends throughout society. Men only deceive themselves if they deny that society is arranged in ranks and classes. "Men of the same habits, the same degree of cultivation and refinement, the same opinions, naturally associate together, in every class of life," Cooper wrote in one book;[1] he noted in another that throughout the American Revolution there was not a solitary instance of a young soldier rising to high command by the mere force of his talents;[2] he thought the Episcopalian form of Christian faith, with its gentle insistance upon hierarchic lines, the only right form of religion in the modern world;[3] and in a striking discussion of "the private duties of station" in *The American Democrat,* after declaring that birth made a difference "even in the most democratical of the American communities," and arguing that "to reduce all to a common level of ignorance and vulgarity . . . would be virtually to return to a condition of barbarism," he asseverated his belief that the gentleman is as necessary to society as the laborer because "knowledge is as necessary to the progress of a people as physical force."[4] Where gentlemen exist,

> the arts are more advanced, and men learn to see that there

[1] *The American Democrat,* edited by H. L. Mencken (New York: Alfred A. Knopf, 1931), p. 75.

[2] *The Chainbearer,* p. 10.

[3] See *Wyandotté: or, The Hutted Knoll,* p. 125; *The Redskins; or, Indian and Injin,* pp. 246-248; *The Crater,* pp. 85, 92-93.

[4] *The American Democrat,* pp. 75, 76, 85.

> are tastes more desirable than those of the mere animal. In such a neighborhood they acquire habits which contribute to their happiness by advancing their intellect, they learn the value of refinement in their intercourse, and obtain juster notions of the nature and of the real extent of their rights. He who would honor learning, and taste, and sentiment, and refinement of every sort, ought to respect its possessors, and, in all things but those which affect rights, defer to their superior advantages . . . They who do not see and feel the importance of possessing a class of such men in a community, to give it tone, a high and far sighted policy, and lofty views in general, can know little of history, and have not reflected on the inevitable consequences of admitted causes . . . happy, indeed, is the nation, in which, power being the common property, there is sufficient discrimination and justice to admit the intelligent and refined to a just participation of its influence.

Great estates, he held, are "generally of more benefit to the community than to their owners," but nevertheless gentlemen keep them up from a spirit of *noblesse oblige,* because property is the ground of moral independence, the means of improving the faculties and of doing good, the agent, in sum, "in all that distinguishes the civilized man from the savage."[1]

But when Cooper returned from Europe in 1833, he came back to a country in which it was no longer possible for a gentleman to attain felicity. The whole theory of the state had been, he thought, falsified. Status was replaced by equality. Property in land, the true basis of republican happiness, had become the excuse for speculation; wealth, which had formerly enabled gentlemen to live liberally for the benefit of the nation, had been overcast by the immorality of getting rich; and Episcopalian Christianity, with its quiet acceptance of rank and class, was lost in an invasion

[1] The same, pp. 85-87, 132.

of Calvinist Yankees, who twisted the doctrine of divine vocation into the gospel of getting on. Political debate had meant the courteous exchange of lofty views; now an unscrupulous press manufactured public opinion and invaded the sanctity of private life. In addition, the law was no longer the embodiment of reason—the populace swarmed over private property, juries failed to convict libelers even at the direction of judges, and a timorous legislature was wiping out ancient estates by passing statutes inspired by demagogues, whom he powerfully pictured in the persons of Steadfast Dodge and Jason Newcome. On the old terms happiness was impossible; and a mounting despair led him to turn his novels into presentations of the lack of faith in God or of the ingratitude of man to man.

Wyandotté (1843) and *The Oak Openings* (1848) are studies in the crisscross of false and true religion, fidelity and treachery. In *The Crater* (1847) the unthinking populace, led by newspaper editors, sectarian religionists, and eloquent demagogues, oust their life-long benefactor, Mark Woolston, who, returning to the United States, thereafter "regarded all popular demonstrations with distaste."[1] *Jack Tier* (1848) is an amazing study of treachery and deception in the sea service, which Cooper had always regarded as the embodiment of fidelity. In *The Sea Lions* (1849) Roswell Gardner, sent to the unknown southern sea by an unscrupulous New Englander, turns Trinitarian in the long Antarctic night, but the conversion is less absurd when one realizes that Cooper is trying to dramatize the truth that for him happiness is now found only in God. And in his last novel, *The Ways of the Hour* (1850), all notions of equity disappear from a fantastic book, wherein the vulgarity and incompetence of the jury system are outsmarted by an insane heroine. Not otherwise, apparently, could he express his profound despair at the breakdown of law.

[1] *The Crater,* Preface, p. v.

A passage in *The Sea Lions* eloquently sums up Cooper's final verdict on American society:

> . . . we hold that it is every hour becoming less and less possible for an American to maintain his rights against numbers. There is no question that the government of this great Republic was intended to be one of well-considered and upright principles, in which certain questions are to be referred periodically to majorities, as the wisest and most natural, as well as the most just mode of disposing of them. Such a government, well administered, and with an accurate observance of its governing principles, would probably be the best that human infirmity will allow men to administer; but when the capital mistake is made of supposing that their numbers are to control all things, regardless of those great fundamental laws that the state has adopted for its own restraint, it may be questioned if so loose, and capricious, and selfish a system, is not in great danger of becoming the very worst scheme of polity that cupidity ever set in motion . . . This influence of numbers, this dire mistake of the very nature of liberty, by placing men and their passions above those great laws of right which come direct from God himself, is increasing in force, and threatens consequences which may set at naught the well-devised schemes of the last generation for the security of the state, and the happiness of that very people, who can never know either security or even peace, until they learn to submit themselves, without a thought of resistance, to those great rules of right which in truth form the *spirit* of their institutions, and which are only too often in opposition to their own impulses and motives.[1]

Where, then, was happiness to be found? Not in the stake-in-society theory of Adam Smith, which Cooper satirized in the story of Sir John Goldencalf in *The Monikins;* and not in the mere getting of money, the emptiness of which he exposed in the life of Deacon Pratt in *The Sea*

[1] *The Sea Lions: or, The Lost Sealers,* pp. 143-144.

Lions. Happiness is rather to be found in the contemplation of God and of His works. In Cooper's later books the universe passes beyond the simplicities which contented Deerslayer and becomes the majestic and mysterious universe of the astronomer, indicative alike of the might, the mystery, and the goodness of God. Two passages published in 1849 must suffice to illustrate the point:

> The physical marvels of the universe produce little more reflection than the profoundest moral truths. A million of eyes shall pass over the firmament, on a cloudless night, and not a hundred minds shall be filled with a proper sense of the power of that dread Being that created all that is there—not a hundred hearts glow with the adoration that such an appeal to the senses and understanding ought naturally to produce.

But—and this is the second passage—

> . . . when health or the usual means of success abandon us, . . . we are made to feel how totally we are insufficient for the achievement of even our own purposes, much less to qualify us to reason on the deep mysteries that conceal the beginning and the end. It has often been said that the most successful leaders of their fellow-men have had the clearest views of their own insufficiency to attain their own objects.[1]

In the God who alone can bring good out of evil and evil out of good, as he tells us in the preface to *The Oak Openings,* Cooper came to place his final hope of felicity.

iii

To pass from Cooper to Emerson is to move out of the Jacksonian era into the world of the anti-slavery movement, the Civil War, and reconstruction. When Emerson was born, Jefferson was still in his first term as president; when he died, Chester A. Arthur lived in the White House. His

[1] The same, Preface, pp. iii, v.

birth coincides with the Louisiana Purchase; at his death, the continental United States had reached its present dimensions and was about to become a great imperial power. Emerson's first book, *Nature,* was published on the verge of the panic year of 1837; his last effective work, *Letters and Social Aims,* was copyrighted in 1875, two years after the panic of 1873. The aging man looked upon an industrial and political order undreamed of by the youth and had experienced a set of military and economic crises greater than those that Cooper knew. What did happiness mean to the sage of Concord amid these mighty convulsions?

It would be easy to say that the answer is simplicity itself. While he was at Harvard, young Emerson wrote in his journal:

> I deliberately shut up my books in a cloudy July noon, put on my old clothes and old hat and slink away to the whortleberry bushes and slip with the greatest satisfaction into a little cowpath where I am sure I can defy observation. This point gained, I solace myself for hours with picking blueberries and other trash of the woods, far from fame, behind the birch-trees. I seldom enjoy hours as I do these. I remember them in winter; I expect them in spring.

And the man of sixty-five confided to his diary in Concord:

> The only place where I feel the joy of eminent domain is in my woodlot. My spirits rise whenever I enter it. I can spend the entire day there with hatchet or pruning-shears making paths, without a remorse of wasting time. I fancy the birds know me, and even the trees make little speeches or hint them.[1]

Humane and charming as these reiterated woodnotes are, they do not, however, speak for the transcendentalist or the shrewd social observer.

[1] *Journals of Ralph Waldo Emerson,* edited by Edward Waldo Emerson and Waldo Emerson Forbes (10 vols.; Boston and New York, 1909-1914), II, 244-245; X, 261.

We begin by noting that with him we leave behind all the eighteenth-century postulates of happiness. Emerson had no interest in landed gentry and evinced a sardonic distrust of the moneyed gentlemen in State Street; he had no faith in orthodox Christian theology and no belief that man-made law is the sacred oracle of reason. He characterized the compact theory of society as a joint-stock company, the members of which agree, for the better securing of his bread to each shareholder, to surrender the liberty and culture of the eater—scarcely a sympathetic metaphor—and since he drily remarked that the State Street interpretation of his philosophy was that it threatened to invalidate contracts, he evidently did not agree with the courts in equating the pursuit of happiness with business life. "Was it that houses and lands, offices, wine, horses, dress, luxury," he said,

> are had by unprincipled men, whilst the saints are poor and despised; and that a compensation is to be made to these last hereafter, by giving them the like gratifications another day,—bank-stock and doubloons, venison and champagne . . . "You sin now, we shall sin by and by; we would sin now, if we could; not being successful, we expect our revenge tomorrow."

In fact, he said,

> there is an instinctive sense, however obscure and yet inarticulate, that the whole constitution of property, on its present tenures, is injurious, and its influence on persons deteriorating and degrading; that truly the only interest for the consideration of the State is persons; that property will always follow persons; that the highest end of government is the culture of men . . .[1]

As for the doctrine of the two callings, or the theory that

[1] *The Works of Ralph Waldo Emerson*, edited by James Elliott Cabot (Standard Library edition; 14 vols.; Boston and New York, 1883-1893), II, 92-93; III, 195-196. From "Compensation," *Essays, First Series*, and "Politics," *Essays, Second Series*.

the righteous man must *eo ipso* be rich and happy, he denied it on the Benjamin Franklin level of the prudential virtues, though, as we shall see, he affirmed it on the higher plane of heroism and fulfillment. In general, he repudiated the axioms of the eighteenth century. "The impoverishing philosophy of ages," he wrote, "has laid stress on the distinctions of the individual, and not on the universal attributes of man,"[1] but the attributes of man for him were not those of the Age of Reason.

These considerations are negative; what, in Emerson's view, was positive happiness? It lay in a joyous sense of individual power, latent or active, streaming from a dynamic centrality which is the Over-Soul, universal mind, or God. Passive felicity, so to speak, might be a private and even a mystical experience, which could occur while you were crossing a bare common, among snow puddles, at twilight, under a clouded sky, or when, in the context of unspoiled nature, you became a transparent eyeball or grew like corn and melons, at once nothing and everything, an autonomous personality, yet part and parcel of God. To this end health was necessary, on which he laid great stress, since it cannot be taught by society but is the product of nature, as the sun-beaten rock teaches firmness to the fisherman. This simple relation to the universe is, however, broken into by a variety of secondary desires—for riches or pleasure or mundane power or human praise, which corrupt man and language. Hence he excoriated the hypocrisy of society, which will not let the individual be himself. He said scornfully:

> Tell me not how great your project is, the civil liberation of the world, its conversion into a Christian church, the establishment of public education, cleaner diet, a new division of labor and of land, laws of love for laws of property;—I say to you plainly there is no end to which

[1] The same, I, 157. From "Literary Ethics" (1838).

> your practical faculty can aim, so sacred or so large, that, if pursued for itself, will not at last become carrion and an offence to the nostril. The imaginative faculty of the soul must be fed with objects immense and eternal . . . always giving health.[1]

With this aspect of Emersonianism one must associate a way of pursuing happiness characteristic of the later nineteenth century—those forms of belief like Christian Science, New Thought, Spiritualism, and Faith Healing, which seek to transcend the ills that flesh is heir to, including doctors, by iterating that the body is transient, matter an illusion, pain an anomaly, and that the soul can, if it will, drink in therapeutic optimism from the wells of the Infinite.

But if Emerson was the enraptured Yankee, the Yankee did not neglect in his rapture the here and now. Happiness in society, with him as with Carlyle, was the opportunity to do the work you were born to do. At first this looks like the doctrine of the two callings, but that theological fusion of religion and selfishness was, he thought, hypocritical:

> The young man, on entering life, finds the way to lucrative employments blocked with abuses. The ways of trade are grown selfish to the borders of theft, and supple to the borders (if not beyond the borders) of fraud. The employments of commerce are not intrinsically unfit for a man, or less genial to his faculties; but these are now in their general course so vitiated by derelictions and abuses at which all connive that . . . every young man . . . must forget the prayers of his childhood and . . . take on the harness of routine and obsequiousness.[2]

If, as he firmly believed, "every man has this call of the power to do somewhat unique, and no man has any other call,"

[1] The same, I, 205. From "The Method of Nature" (1838).
[2] The same, I, 220-221. From "Man the Reformer" (1841).

> the pretence that he has another call, a summons by name and personal election and outward 'signs . . . ,' is fanaticism, and betrays obtuseness to perceive that there is one mind in all the individuals, and no respect of persons therein.[1]

Thus quietly destroying both the economic and the theological basis of laissez-faire, he put forth simultaneously a positive theory.

Happiness, or at least social satisfaction, must come from a renewal of the sense of dignity and craftsmanship in labor, that "study of the external world," as he called it, which is far more important than money-getting. Therefore, for him, labor was "God's education."

> Every man ought to stand in primary relations with the work of the world; ought to do it himself, and not to suffer the accident of his having a purse in his pocket, or his having been bred to some dishonorable and injurious craft, to sever him from those duties . . .[2]

In this grander view even a mercantile aristocracy lacked permanence. Calling is character, not money. He wrote in opposition to a low theory of prudence and the mean qualities of the theory of the division of labor—entrance into the business world, he said, shrinks young men. "For you, O broker," he said in the essay entitled "Circles,"

> there is no other principle but arithmetic. For me, commerce is of trivial import; love, faith, truth of character, the aspiration of men, these are sacred . . . If a man should dedicate himself to the payment of notes, would not this be injustice? Does he owe no debt but money?[3]

"I look on that man as happy," he said, "who, when there is a question of success, looks into his work for a reply, not into the market, not into opinion, not into patronage."[4]

1 The same, II, 134. From "Spiritual Laws," *Essays, First Series.*
2 The same, I, 229. From "Man the Reformer."
3 The same, II, 295. In *Essays, First Series.*
4 The same, VI, 215. From "Worship" in *The Conduct of Life.*

> There is no persuasion in the soul of man that he is here for cause, that he was put down in this place by the Creator to do the work for which he inspires him, that thus he is an overmatch for all antagonists that could combine against him.[1]

Enjoying "frolic health,"[2] and fulfilling this spiritual law, that man will be happy who can meet the testing questions:

> *Who are you? What do you? Can you obtain what you wish? Is there method in your consciousness? Can you see tendency in your life? Can you help any soul?* . . . Happy if you can answer them mutely in the order and disposition of your life! Happy for more than yourself, a benefactor of men, if you can answer them in works of wisdom, art, or poetry; bestowing on the general mind of men organic creations, to be the guidance and delight of all who know them. These questions speak to Genius, to that power which is underneath and greater than all talent, and which proceeds out of the constitution of every man . . . whose private counsels are not tinged with selfishness, but are laws.[3]

His theory of self-fulfillment owes something to Locke and Jefferson and vaguely foreshadows William James's definition of the self.

This lofty doctrine of happiness calls forth two observations. The first is that, whatever indirect support it gave to the judicial definition of pursuing happiness, it principally affected American life in fields remote from the law. The doctrine that the law of happiness is self-fulfillment of one's individual genius has taken powerful hold upon education and the arts. In education it offers philosophic support for the elective system under which—and there is much to be said for the idea—not what culture or society requires, but what the individual demands for his own

[1] The same, VII, 257. From "Courage" in *Society and Solitude.*
[2] The same, VIII, 43. From "Creation" in *Poetry and Imagination.*
[3] The same, X, 270. From "The Scholar."

genius became the central principle. In the arts, not imitation, not decorum, not the statement of what oft was thought but ne'er so well expressed—such principles have long ceased to be the canons of success, and have been replaced by self-expression. The happiness of creation is thus sufficiently justified.

> I celebrate myself, and sing myself,
> And what I assume you shall assume,

sang the greatest poet influenced by Emerson; and the doctrine that the happiness of the creator, but not necessarily the happiness of the observer, the auditor, or the reader in receiving the communication of the artist, is the governing consideration—this, in surprising degree, is our modern principle. I am far from saying that Emerson is responsible for American romanticism or for much current psychology; I merely observe that whether he was or was not the classical dualist praised by American neo-humanism, his theory of happiness as self-fulfillment according to spiritual laws, when the spiritual laws disappear, is easily translated into the doctrine that self-expression is self-fulfillment and therefore happiness.

My second observation is that Emerson's attack on business and the businessman preludes an enormous library of fiction which portrays the American businessman as unhappy. In Howells, in James, in Frank Norris, in Jack London, in Sinclair Lewis, in the novels of J. P. Marquand, we have the fictional working out of Emerson's theory that going into business shrinks young men. The incapacity of business life to fulfill one's dream of happiness is the point in characters as remote from each other as Mark Twain's Beriah Sellers, Sinclair Lewis's Babbitt, and the Great Gatsby of F. Scott Fitzgerald. Indeed, so powerful is this tradition that stories which do celebrate the satisfactions of a business career—like the smartness of Get-Rich-Quick

Wallingford, the tales of O. Henry, or the comedies of Harry Leon Wilson—are, we instinctively feel, inferior literature. The queer aftermath of these attacks upon business by Emerson and Cooper is an extraordinary split in our culture; on the one hand, in the eyes of academic schools of commerce, business has risen to the dignity of a profession, and in the eyes of the Rotary Club, the National Association of Manufacturers, and the Luce publications, to question the assumption that business creates happiness is the ultimate *lèse majesté;* on the other hand, most of our writers of serious fiction, a great many painters and cartoonists, and even some satirical musicians are firmly of the opinion that wherever else the pursuit of happiness may lead us, it cannot lead us with hope of success into industry, banking, advertising, manufacture, or commerce.

iv

William James delivered the address at the Emerson Centenary Celebration at Concord in 1903. It was an appropriate choice. The pragmatist owed much to the transcendentalist. "The reading of the divine Emerson," he wrote in a letter,

> has done me a lot of good, and, strange to say, has thrown a strong practical light on my path. The incorruptible way in which he followed his own vocation of seeing such truths as the Universal Soul vouchsafed him . . . and reporting them in the right literary form . . . refusing to be entangled with irrelevancies . . . seems to me a moral lesson to all men who have any genius, however small, to foster.[1]

Like Emerson, James had no patience with the block universe of either metaphysics or theology; like Emerson, he declared that "the real thing to aim at is the liberation

1 *The Letters of William James,* edited by Henry James (2 vols.; Boston [1920]), II, 190. The letter is to Henry James, May 3, 1903.

of the inner interests" of the soul;[1] like Emerson, he experienced moments of mystical rapture, one of which he perfectly describes in a letter to his wife in 1898:

> I spent a good deal of [the night] in the woods, where the streaming moonlight lit up things in a magical checkered play, and it seemed as if the Gods of all the nature-mythologies were holding an indescribable meeting in my breast with the moral Gods of the inner life. . . The intense significance of some sort, of the whole scene, if one could only *tell* the significance; the intense inhuman remoteness of its inner life, and yet the intense *appeal* of it; its everlasting freshness and its immemorial antiquity and decay; its utter Americanism, and every sort of patriotic suggestiveness, and you, and my relation to you part and parcel of it all, and beaten up with it, so that memory and sensation all whirled inexplicably together; it was indeed worth coming for . . . one of the happiest lonesome nights of existence, and I understand now what a poet is.[2]

The Emersonian doctrine of the individual's relation to the Over-Soul anticipates and parallels the Jamesian doctrine, set forth in the essay on the energies of man, that human beings use only a small part of the powers they possess. Moreover, James's sardonic view of the theory that business success means happiness is as corrosive as Emerson's:

> Who that has travelled in Europe is not familiar with the type of the broken-down American business-man, sent abroad to recruit his collapsed nervous system? With his haggard, hungry mien, unfitted by life-long habit for taking any pleasure in passive contemplation, and with too narrow a culture to be interested in the historical or aesthetic side of what meets his eye, he tries to cheat the *tedium vitae* by a feverish locomotion, and seems to draw a ghostly com-

[1] William James, *Memories and Studies* (New York and London, 1911), pp. 89-90.

[2] *Letters*, II, 76-77. July 9, 1898.

> fort from a peevish and foolish criticism of everything he meets—the tyranny of despots, the dinginess of the old paintings, and the mendacity of the natives, the absence of the ballot-box, the crookedness of the streets, the fearful waste of raw material in walls, harnesses, and conveyances, and the barbarousness of the window fastenings.[1]

Finally, the Jamesian view of truth as something whose meaning is determined by the conduct it is fitted to produce parallels the Emersonian varieties of spiritual experience in subtle and unexpected ways.

Our present inquiry, however, is not into the history of metaphysics but into the meaning of happiness; and here James represents the end of a long tradition. If, for example, either social or private happiness results from the correspondence of human life to immutable reason—the Blackstone theory—you cannot, if you are persuaded by James's *Pragmatism* (1907) or his *A Pluralistic Universe* (1909), any longer adhere to this notion of either law or truth. If prosperity and happiness are guaranteed by Christian theology to the religious man, you cannot, after reading James's *The Varieties of Religious Experience* (1902), hold quite the same belief in theology that you had before. And if happiness means the acceptance of things on the basis of right reason, as the eighteenth century believed, the place of rationality in consciousness is so considerably shrunken by a study of James's *The Principles of Psychology* (1890), especially the chapters on habit, reasoning, the stream of thought, and the consciousness of self, that Locke seems for a time to be a mere museum piece.

To say that James was ever the physiological psychologist is not to say that he was only a physiological psychologist, but reminds us that for him, whatever else life might be, it was the never-ending adjustment of inner

[1] "Vacations," *The Nation,* XVII (August 7, 1873), 90.

experience and outer world. In this dynamic centrality, concepts lost their boundaries, values ran into each other, desire colored truth and truth, desire. Self became "the sum total of all that a man *can* call his," not only his body and psychic powers, but his clothes and his house, his wife and children, and so on.[1] Thus psychic life extended outward. But in addressing ministerial associations on the theme that there is no hostility to theism in the hypothesis that the basis of thinking must be physiological, he showed that material existence extended, so to say, inward. For him the strong mark of rationality was found in a resultant emotional tone; the transition out of a state of puzzle and perplexity into rational comprehension was, he said, a transition into a state of "lively relief and pleasure," and he found rationality always accompanied by "a strong feeling of ease, peace, and rest."[2] All this suggested to him that nineteenth-century psychology needed to become a science, and that it might become one by throwing off its metaphysical and its theological clothing; so that, when one abandoned the presuppositions of metaphysics and theology, and examined mental operations as they truly are, all sorts of new elements entered the problem. Take, for example, rationalism, which in the abstract, he says, means four things: definitely statable abstract principles; definite facts of sensation; definite hypotheses based on such facts; and definite inferences logically drawn. But James goes on:

> If we look on man's whole mental life as it exists, on the life of men that lies apart from their learning and science, and that they inwardly and privately follow, we have to confess that the part of it of which rationalism can give an account is relatively superficial. It is the part that has

[1] *The Principles of Psychology* (2 vols.; New York, 1890), I, 291.

[2] *Collected Essays and Reviews* (New York and London, 1920), p. 84. From "The Sentiment of Rationality."

> the *prestige* undoubtedly, for it has the loquacity, it can challenge you for proofs, and chop logic, and put you down with words. But it will fail to convince or convert you all the same, if your dumb intuitions are opposed to its conclusions. If you have intuitions at all, they come from a deeper level of your nature than the loquacious level which rationalism inhabits. Your whole subconscious life, your impulses, your faiths, your needs, your divinations, have prepared the premises, of which your consciousness now feels the weight of the result; and something in you absolutely *knows* that the result must be truer than any logic-chopping rationalistic talk, however clear, that may contradict it.[1]

In a letter discussing *The Varieties of Religious Experience,* the book from which I have just quoted, he says that he has deliberately cut himself off in this study from theologies and scholasticisms, which have "no proper *intellectual* deliverance of their own, but belong to a region deeper, and more vital and practical, than that which the intellect inhabits." "*We* cannot," he says in the book itself, "divide man sharply into an animal and a rational part. *We* cannot distinguish natural from supernatural effects." And in the letter he continues:

> I attach the mystical or religious consciousness to the possession of an extended subliminal self, with a thin partition through which messages make irruption. We are thus made convincingly aware of the presence of a sphere of life larger and more powerful than our usual consciousness, with which the latter is nevertheless continuous. The impressions and impulsions and emotions and excitements which we thence receive help us to live, they found invincible assurance of a world beyond the sense, they melt our hearts and communicate significance and value to everything and make us happy.[2]

[1] *The Varieties of Religious Experience* (New York and London, 1902), p. 73.

[2] *Letters,* II, 149-150 (to Henry W. Rankin, June 16, 1901); *The Varieties of Religious Experience,* p. 327.

In sum, all that philosophy and theology—and for that matter, economics and political science and theories of ethics—can do is, therefore, to give conceptual interpretations of an experiential life, but until the subliminal consciousness is content, happiness is not possible. Answering a questionaire about his religious belief, he consistently wrote that to him God was but "dimly [real]" and that spirituality was "susceptibility to ideals, but with a certain freedom to indulge in imagination about them. . . Otherwise you have mere morality, or 'taste.' " "I can't possibly pray," he declared, "I feel foolish and artificial;"[1] and conversion, which usually means the attainment of some form of religious happiness, seemed to him on the whole the subconscious incubation of some new center of psychological energy, which by and by bursts into flower, overflows, suffuses old pathways in both the subconscious and the conscious mind. Whatever we are is mysterious: "our interests, our tendencies of attention, our motor impulses, the aesthetic, moral, and theoretic combinations we delight in, the extent of our power of apprehending schemes of relation . . . have all grown up in ways of which at present we can give no account"; but whatever we are, we are unshakeably attached to our own nervous structures. Yet

> there are resources in us that naturalism with its literal and legal virtues never recks of, possibilities that take our breath away, of another kind of happiness and power, based on giving up our own will and letting something higher work for us, and these seem to show a world wider than either physics or philistine ethics can imagine . . . our natural experience, our strictly moralistic and prudential experience, may be only a fragment of real human experience.[2]

[1] *Letters,* II, 214.
[2] *A Pluralistic Universe* (New York and London, 1909), pp. 305-306.

What, then, is happiness for William James? The universe of discourse in which Jefferson moved was one which, in this passage, James expressly repudiates. Not moralistic or prudential experiences alone, but something other is needed. Happiness is a compound of temperament and adjustment. In the great chapters on the religion of healthy-mindedness he points out that there are those who are born happy or who easily acquire happiness, who revel in "the sort of religion which consists in a grateful admiration for the gift of so happy an existence."[1] And he noted how New Thought, Mind Cure, the social gospel, and the religion of happiness had diverted preachers from the condemnation of sin to the belittling of it. Some exhorted their flocks to get rid of the martyr habit, and for others religion become a form of mental therapy, a kind of amateur psychological study of its own.

For those not thus fortunate, for those to whom the world is painful in its moral and material expression, happiness is a problem of adjustment—that same sort of adjustment which is the stock-in-trade of psychiatry today. If the universe is not moral, we owe it no allegiance, we are free to "follow no law but that of prudence in coming to terms with such of her particular features as will help us to our private ends."[2] Optimism is as true as pessimism in the world at large; but optimism of an intelligent sort, has at least this advantage, that

> the facts of the world are a fit basis for the *summum bonum,* if we do our share and react upon them as it is meant we should (with fortitude, for example, and undismayed hope).[3]

1 *The Varieties of Religious Experience,* p. 78.

2 *The Will to Believe and Other Essays in Popular Philosophy* (New York and London, 1912), p. 44.

3 *Collected Essays,* pp. 18-19.

Fortitude and undismayed hope are precisely the assumptions in our treatment today of the abnormal, the melancholy, the unhappy—in short, the maladjusted—and when James tells us that

> the world is thus absolutely good only in a potential or hypothetic sense, and the hypothetic form of the optimistic belief is the very signature of its consistency, and the first condition of its probability,[1]

he charters both professional and popular psychiatry, with their doctrine of adjustment.

Because we Americans are so generally the cultural offspring of William James, we are likely to murmur, "Well, happiness as adjustment is no novelty." Thus we fail to understand how radical is James's empiricism in this field. Happiness defined as adjustment between an inner world more subliminal than rational and an outer world partially but principally brute matter would have been incomprehensible to virtually every other writer we have examined. To the ancients the cosmic drama, if intelligible, was so apart and aloof that the sole possibility of felicity lay in the spectator theory of happiness. For the scholastics the play was written, the parts cast, the tragedy that of man, the hero the conqueror worm except for a *deus ex machina.* Human beings were scarcely call-boys in that theater. For the Age of Reason man was equipped with rational faculties to keep his passions in order, in a universe of clear design and mechanical perfection; consequently, happiness, whether conceived as political, economic, or social planning, was so definite an intellectual concept that courts could determine what made men unhappy. Even for Emerson happiness was possible for Everyman in cosmic abundance, since all Everyman had to do was to polarize himself on the Over-Soul. But while

[1] The same, p. 19.

nineteenth-century judicial decisions were ponderously enforcing the economic system of Adam Smith; while American pulpits were rationally demonstrating that in modern theology the truth, "Many are called and few are chosen," should have its wording reversed; and while scientists like Agassiz were anxiously trying to think both God's thoughts and Darwin's after them, James was quietly altering the whole theory. Men, he said in effect, do not pursue happiness as a right, they come to it as a necessity, either by adjusting themselves to the world, or by adjusting the world to themselves. So wonderfully has our concept of happiness altered that insanity, which was once either a divine possession or a divine affliction, now has nothing to do with theology and everything to do with adjustment; partly because, as James insisted in his seminars, "there is no sharp line to be drawn between 'healthy' and 'unhealthy' minds."[1] I suspect Mr. Jefferson would have denied this statement.

Nevertheless, as I have two or three times insisted, the Jamesian doctrine of the self—"the sum total of all that a man *can* call his"—relates him to the Lockeian doctrine of property-happiness: "that property which men have in their persons as well as goods." Not what I am but what I own, what I have made my own, this is for James the essential *me*. Not what I own, but the faculty to make use of my own, the liberty to employ my faculties to ends I have myself determined—this, says Locke, is the higher meaning of *property*. Add to these as a middle term the Emersonian doctrine of self-development which is to result in "bestowing on the general mind of men organic creations, to be the guidance and delight of all who know them," and you have our twentieth-century inheritance. That inheritance, passing into a realm remote from courts of law, has, in some sense, translated the problem

1 Dickinson S. Miller's comment, quoted in *Letters,* II, 15.

of the right to happiness out of ethics, out of law, and out of religion into a problem of both national and individual psychology, normal or otherwise as events might prove. Let us in conclusion scrutinize the results.

V

The Technique of Happiness

IF ONE LOOKS only at the surface of life, the United States seems to be contentedly pursuing happiness. In a famous phrase William Dean Howells once murmured that the smiling aspects of life are the more American; and though his words are commonly quoted out of context and made to apply to Howells rather than to the novelists he was ironically describing, he did say that though we have death in America as well as a great deal of disease which the multiplicity of our patent medicines does not seem to cure, the tragedy is not unique, and the large, cheerful average of health and success and happy life is distinctly national. So it seemed in 1891; whether Howells would find it so sixty years later is anybody's guess. I incline to think he would. Indeed, it is precisely because we feel national happiness is threatened, that our anxieties increase.

Despite our tensions, the United States remains a happy land, the land of good cheer, God's country. It produces the Optimists' Club, the glad books, the Boosters' society, manuals on how to attain peace of mind, songs to the effect that though I want to be happy, I can't be happy unless you are happy too, and office posters saying: If you can't boost, don't knock. We print cards concerning miles and miles of smiles, we look at cartoons showing little Mr. New Year radiantly kicking out old Mr. Gloom, and our mottoes declare that it ain't no use to grumble and complain when it's just as cheap and easy to rejoice. The idea spreads to many departments of life. In the nineteenth century statesmen were statesmen and took a statesman's stance, but beginning with Teddy Roosevelt's teeth, our presidents have radiated gladness—Taft's chuckle, Wilson's fondness for limericks, Harding's geniality, Coolidge's Yankee witticisims, F.D.R.'s smile, Harry Truman's grin. The omission in this distinguished line is Herbert Hoover, who remains in folklore the false prophet bringing in depression; and it is illuminating to remember that the least humorous of the list, Woodrow Wilson, is likewise tagged with defeat. Parenthetically one notes that the only vice-president aging voters remember as such is the man who got off the wisecrack about the five-cent cigar.

Advertisements reveal our folkways. They prove that the effect of purchasing American cigarets, oil furnaces, laxatives, shirts, automobiles, house paint, television sets, coffee, nylon stockings, vacuum cleaners, chewing gum, coated paper, electric trains, and dog food is the instant creation of felicity. Looking at the smiles on the faces of salesmen depicted in these pictures, you wonder what the vintners buy one-half so precious as the things they sell. On our billboards the disappearance of a car going sixty miles an hour awakens excited grins on the faces of those it has just endangered, beer is drunk with the utmost affability by even a solitary toper, gum-chewers flash white teeth, and the effect of toothpaste on a visage three feet high surpasses the efforts of Rubens.

I have taken the trouble to count the human beings depicted in advertisements printed in a single issue of a single national weekly, including every face the features of which I can distinguish. Out of 257 faces in the advertisements, about 178 are smiling, grinning, laughing, or chuckling; an additional fourteen are singing; and three are smiling through their tears. Five animals are depicted with broad grins. There remain sixty-odd unsmiling countenances, but let no one be depressed. Of these, three are those of persons peacefully asleep; three belong to men contentedly blowing smoke-rings; and about two dozen are the faces of enraptured children or of infants. I by-pass six Arabs, who in the nature of things cannot participate in American felicity, to note that some of the frowning faces are comic, and that others are halves of a before-and-after equation, the companionate visages being jollity incarnate. In these advertisements an upset toboggan produces only gaiety, a man up a tree with a saw is filled with joy, a mechanic carrying a can of engine sludge registers innocent merriment, a housewife pushing a vacuum cleaner bursts into song, and four salesmen of a storage battery join in a quartet. The most incredible of these pictures shows a man in evening clothes peering at his rapturous wife through the window of a de luxe sedan while he stands in a sleet storm, his face one broad, genial smile.

This happy breed of men inhabits a world in which idleness is a pleasure and labor a bore. Once upon a time woman's work was never done, but in the advertising she toils not, neither does she spin. Our prepared meat loaf is easy-slicing, easy-eating. Just add milk. Here are the easiest cookies of all. It's no bother to make creamed dishes and creamed sauces. Mix your banana cake in three minutes. All you do is put in the water and coffee. Simply pour the batter into a pan and bake. New wonder method makes jams and jellies in fifteen minutes. Your baby will clean the plate and lick the spoon.

Nor are these Arabian Nights visions culinary only. All household chores are done in the same opiate dream. Free of the usual messy refrigerator chores, you never bother with defrosting. Our washing machine saves you work—just a touch of the finger-tip starts, stops, reverses, and releases the rollers. Most American families have had to wash more than 18,615 dishes a year, but now you need never hand-wash or dry piles of dishes again. Keep your silver bright without polishing. In a matter of moments you can make your bathroom a model of safety and smartness. Cuts ironing in half. Slips over baby's head so conveniently. Putting on chintz is easier than painting, it just takes scissors and paste. Buttons are no problem: no tools! no paste! no sewing! just snip the fabric, place it over the buttons, and snap. Because my gas range is automatic, I can go out with Al when he is on leave and still come home to a perfectly cooked meal.

Remembering that girdles have never been so young, so utterly freedom-loving as these, the designers of which have searched the world over and then priced them sweet and low, Al's wife goes forth, her eyes sparkling with somebody's drops, her lips aglow with lipstick, her skin cleansed by a soap thirty-six specialists after 1285 tests proved would make a lovelier complexion in fourteen days, her stockings held up by a garter pantie of specially knit nylons, her hair lustrous from a shampoo that played its vital part in the fabulous glamor-career of a (named) sweetheart of screen and radio, her figure slimmer than ever because she has lost weight in the quick, natural way nature intended her to, and blowing her nose, if she has to, on somebody's tissue, which serves but one, saves as it serves, and doesn't need washing.

Doubtless social psychologists and cultural anthropologists can tell us what deep-seated need in the national psyche this notion of happiness exists to satisfy. I am content to note how completely it reverses the traditional American belief that there is discomfort in idleness, solid satisfaction in industry. Perhaps we can measure how far we have come. In 1758 Benjamin Franklin published "The Way to Wealth," a catena of folk wisdom, to show that happiness and industry are interchangeable. Here is a characteristic paragraph:

> Methinks I hear some of you say, 'Must a man afford himself no leisure?' I will tell thee, my friend, what Poor Richard says: *Employ thy time well, if thou meanest to gain leisure; and, since thou art not sure of a minute, throw not away an hour.* Leisure is time for doing something useful; this leisure the diligent man will obtain, but the lazy man never; for *A life of leisure and a life of laziness are two things. Many, without labor, would live by their wits only, but they break for want of stock;* whereas industry gives comfort and plenty and respect. *Fly pleasures, and they will follow you.*[1]

This is not from a Puritan minister but from a man who smugly applied to himself the Biblical verse: "Seest thou a man diligent in business? He shall stand before kings." Nowadays leisure is a serious problem of import to sociology.[2]

Happiness is not reserved for adults alone; it has another extensive kingdom, this time for the young. The belief that happiness is a primary right, or duty, or element, or condition of life now conditions American books for children. A hundred years ago death was conventionally a regular part of the formula for juvenile literature. Sometime—as in a book on my shelves entitled *Little Emily the Peacemaker*—the book existed only that the child might die; and this formula, transferred to a larger frame of reference, helps explain the immense popularity in this country of Paul Dombey and Little Nell. Even in that astonishingly modern masterpiece, *Little Women,* the King of Terrors hovers over Beth and finally gets her.

But it was not death alone that confronted the young reader in these fictions. He learned a good many sobering

[1] *The Works of Benjamin Franklin,* edited by John Bigelow (12 vols.; New York and London, 1904), II, 30-31.

[2] See the lengthy discussion of the problem of leisure at the Corning Conference, in *Creating an Industrial Civilization,* edited by Eugene Staley (New York: Harper and Bros., 1952).

facts about life as well. Father's illness, or the mysterious loss of the family's capital, or papa's temporary removal from business and the domestic hearth was made the occasion for instilling into father's little flock the truths that life is real, life is earnest, and that son or daughter was supposed to act, heart within and God o'erhead. In other stories the widowed sempstress was aided in keeping a decent cottage roof over her head by the help, often providential, always unsolicited, of some child, who was thus simultaneously learning the pleasures of approbation and the grimmer law of wages. Sometimes, of course, unexpected relief was brought to her, especially if she had tuberculosis, through the grave-eyed little daughter of a rich but Christian family recently moved into the neighborhood. The ragged newsboy may have been cheerful, but he had to work all day long; and if the son of wealthy parents had a pony, he jolly well had to take care of it or the little beast would throw him. In sum, poverty, struggle, illness, disappointment, and death—all that the twentieth century thinks of as "frustration"—were formerly commonplace elements in imaginative literature for the young. Not the pursuit of happiness but the duties of industry, frugality, manly respect for the weak, and a sober Christian altruism were the "notes" of this writing.

A hundred years has changed all this. Children's books are now almost wholly dedicated to happiness.[1] They are written in what I may call the *Wizard of Oz* formula. I have no desire to throw off on this enchanting masterpiece, but nevertheless L. Frank Baum invented a world in which everything is something else. That something else is a happy, happy something else. Thus in the beginning of the story a prodigious natural catastrophe snatches little Dorothy and her dog from the plains of Kansas and pre-

[1] I did not encounter David Riesman's absorbing analysis of contemporary juvenile literature until after these lectures were delivered. See his *The Lonely Crowd* (New Haven: Yale University Press, 1950), especially Part I, chap. iv.

sumably kills her industrious relatives, but the hard-working aunt and uncle are not really dead, and Dorothy is not in the slightest danger. She has merely been translated to the country of Oz, a sort of juvenile Land of Cockaigne. Through this delightful landscape winds a road of brick, but it is not composed of common paving brick, dirtied by horses and automobile sludge, it is made of shining yellow brick, golden in its sheen, and gold, as everyone knows, is the color of happiness. Down the whole length of this road Dorothy and her companions walk for days on end without ever getting really tired (as, for example, Miss Alcott's *Little Men* get both tired and cross). Food is always provided, and there is always a good place to sleep.

Dorothy meets a lion, but the lion is not in the least the savage beast of the desert, he is a cowardly lion, or rather he proves in the end to be so innocently brave, he does not know how courageous he is. She also meets a scarecrow, but the scarecrow is not really a bundle of filth, he is the cleverest fellow in the group. She meets a tin woodman, but this conception, which is essentially frightening as Frankenstein's monster or Karel Capek's robot is frightening, does not scare even a child, since the tin woodman is at once translated into a benevolent uncle with a heart of gold.

Wicked witches are crushed to death without agony, unlike wicked witches in Grimm's fairy tales, who really die with a shriek. When Dorothy finally unmasks the tremendous Wizard of Oz, he proves to be Casper Milquetoast, and wouldn't harm a fly. During the whole course of the story Dorothy is never in the slightest danger, not even the fairy-tale danger of Hansel and Gretel, or Rumpelstilskin, or Little Red Ridinghood, or Jack, up the beanstalk. Nor does she do anything except trust in the universe. As there is a movement to erase from juvenile literature such dangerous thoughts as Jack's getting cooked, or Little Red Ridinghood's getting eaten, or Hansel's getting roasted, lest these images create unhappiness in the buried psyche of the adult-about-to-be, the contrast of little Dorothy's facile success—a dream in little of going to Hollywood—is the more striking. Neither the child heroine nor the child reader is called upon to confront misfortune, or wickedness, or labor, or death. All these things are illusory. They continue to be illusory. From the little ferry-boat that went to sea with a broad grin on its pilot-house face, to Ferdinand, who only wanted to smell the flowers, the Wizard of Oz formula prevails. Small wonder the children lap up crime in the television shows, where life is bracing and vigorous.

These books, of course, are not manufactured for children. Children do not buy books. Books are bought for them by adults, who give them away, and in giving them necessarily project upon children their notions of the world of the child. It seems a fair inference that the cult of happiness in children's books has less to do with children and more to do with adult fantasy than the simplicities of children's librarians are prepared to admit. The lost Atlantis of our youth is a common enough figment in many cultures; I suspect that it has never before been so thoroughly commercialized.

The struggle to maintain the fiction that childhood is happiness may be seen in yet another characteristic folkway: the identification of social intercourse with having a good time. When son or daughter returns at two in the morning from a party, the only question an anxious parent may properly ask is: "Did you have a good time?" The answer may be a grunt or an outburst of feminine ecstasy, neither of which proves that the respondent enjoyed himself (or herself) but only that he (or she) recognizes the inquiry as within the rules of the game. To confess that one did not have a good time is to confess utter defeat. It means that one is not popular, and popularity consists in so pursuing happiness at a party that the pleasure of meeting and enjoying A is immediately ended by the intrusion of B, and that in turn by the intrusions of C, D, E, and so on. If I use the feminine formula involving cutting in at dances, there is, of course, an alternative formula for the male, which is to throw the sultan's handkerchief in succession at an indefinite number of beauties. (Contrariwise, of course, one can be completely absorbed by a single glamorous partner, to the exclusion of the world.) Mostly a good time is the incessant pursuing, obtaining, and by-passing an indefinite number of pleasures on the Benthamite principle, slightly modified, that the greatest happiness consists in the greatest possible numbers. If one is so fortunate as to have one of these gifted beings as a member of his family, all other attributes fade in comparison with the supreme truth that George (or May) is so popular—that is, gifted in the pursuit of happiness as a good time.

As any parent knows who has prepared an adolescent daughter for her first "formal," the mere thought of not being popular and of not having a good time—that is, of not being incessantly moved from male to male—brings forth a flood of tears. In actuality the wallflower is one of the most miserable of American females. Deans of women in our colleges might, if they would, make the national hair curl (or uncurl, as fashion dictates) by reciting what they know about girls who come up to college and fail, not in the realm of the intellect, but in the pursuit of happiness. A little reading in the columns of advice to women—mostly younger women—which help to make our newspapers incredible, reveals that the loss and reconquest of popularity by any cunning device of dress, conduct, scent, or make-up are the incessant quest of these writings. Likewise it is canonical for business firms to keep their employees happy, and a good time is had by all just before Christmas, when employer and employee meet on a democratic plane of pursuing pleasure instead of profit. Then even the most unattractive filing clerk is, for once, not to be ignored.

The contrast between the European café, which is a place for leisurely and often solitary meditation, and American café society, wherein to be solitary is to be doomed, emphasizes not only the truth that in this country we pursue a good time, but also the truth that we pursue it in packs. The American roadhouse, country club, dancing place, or other exemplar of highway culture, commercially dedicated to the creation of a good time (if necessary, by the mechanical aid of juke boxes and pinball machines) again contrasts with the European pub or inn, the aim of which is less strenuous enjoyment, even though on festal occasions it may be noisy. A younger American who likes walking, or quiet conversation, or the philosophic delights of reading is more likely to be a source of anxiety than of pride, so removed is he from the good-time formula, whereas in Europe, or what remains of it, such interests and such conduct would be regarded not only as normal but as civilized.

But perhaps our obsession with the good time is nowhere more strikingly revealed than in American church life. "Have a good time at the Y" is a sign that is not infrequent in our cities; it is with a start that one realizes the "Y" in question is the Young Men's (or the Young Women's) *Christian* Association, which in popular speech has dropped religion for youth. American churches were formerly dedicated to individual salvation, but they have turned out to be institutions dedicated, since the vogue of the social gospel, to maintaining a good time more decorous than that of the country club but not essentially different. The young people's meeting, the ladies' aid, the church supper, the church gymnasium, and even the church dance are characteristic contributions to theology. A wholly American invention like the Mormon church does this sort of thing very well, indeed. And these activities have arisen in the most laudable way. Why should the devil have all the good tunes? Why drive young people to cabarets and dance halls when the church parlors are available? The argument is irresistible, but it does not conceal the assumption that the promise of a good time is more potent than the promise of relief from sin. Protestant churches are now customarily open for meditation and prayer, but the meditators are few, and if you really want to see the plant in operation, come around when the young people are having their roller-skating party. Nor is this shift in value confined to the young. Not only do ministers fail to mention hell to ears polite, they fail to mention hell at all. The terrors of death are gone—consider the implication of so American a concept as "Funeral Home." Heaven has also quietly disappeared, partly as a result of the kind of ridicule Mark Twain showered on it in "Captain Stormfield's Visit to Heaven," partly because the idea of beatitude is so antithetic to the idea of a good time had by all that an eternity of endless hymns is essentially meaningless.

ii

"In this democracy," wrote Dorothy Thompson in 1941, "it has become a public duty to be as happy as one can be."[1] One can take happiness thus seriously, but the thoughtful observer is more likely to feel that the examples I have cited come from a world of half-truths and fantasy. The unreality of that world I can best illustrate by citing

[1] Dorothy Thompson, "The Right to Happiness," *Ladies' Home Journal*, LVIII (April 1941), 6.

the purpose of a lecture foundation in one of our older colleges. The unfortunate incumbent is required annually to demonstrate to the young that life is a glad opportunity. No lecturer in recent years has succeeded.

It is, however, more important to note that a profound disharmony exists between the world I have been describing and the world reported by our imaginative writers. These reports altered importantly about thirty years ago. Up to our entry into World War I, the happy ending was standard in novel and stage play, so much so that H. H. Boyesen complained of the iron virgin who strangled art in her maidenly arms. Today the happy ending is chiefly confined to the slick magazines, from whose advertising I have quoted. The well-made play that usually came out all right until the triumph of Eugene O'Neill when the twenties began, is now transmogrified into the formula, boy meets girl—boy loses girl—boy gets girl, on the screen and in television. Radio soap opera is, of course, full of tears, but one has only to mention *A Streetcar Named Desire* to measure the immense distance between glycerine on the air-waves and glycerine on Broadway. In radio scripts nobody grows old, nobody gets locked up in an insane aslyum, nobody dies, and nobody changes.

Such, however, is not the report on American life by serious poets, novelists, and playwrights, if the critics select the right authors as representative of the age. Ours is the waste-land, the lost generation, the lonely crowd, the neurotic personality of our time. Our ordinary fictional successes include *The Lost Week-end, The Snake Pit, The Naked and the Dead,* and *From Here to Eternity.* From Stephen Crane's bewildered and aimless infantryman in *The Red Badge of Courage* through the unhappy lives of *Three Soldiers* to the homosexual tensions of *Guard of Honor,* the descent is steady. The Chicago of Dreiser's early novels was drab enough, but the darkness deepened when James T. Farrell wrote the Studs Lonigan trilogy, it became blackest midnight in Richard Wright's *Native Son,* and though greater misery seemed impossible, this book was followed by Nelson Algren's *The Man with the Golden Arm,* winner of the 1950 National Book Award, a novel of which *Time* magazine wrote: "Readers with queasy stomachs may shrink from an environment in which the unbelievably sordid has become a way of life," an environment inhabited by "a wretched, confused and hopelessly degenerate cast of characters."[1] The genial South of Joel Chandler Harris, Thomas Nelson Page, and F. Hopkinson Smith has vanished, so much so that when, in *John Brown's Body,* Stephen Vincent Benet properly revived the plantation legend in his picture of Wingate Hall, critics complained of its sentimentality. Why not? The South in literature today is tenanted by Popeye, Joe Christmas, Temple Drake, and the unpleasant offspring of the Compson and Sutpen families of Mr. William Faulkner, whose fearsome personalities would seem to prophesy the downfall of a civilization rather than its triumph, especially when one adds to them the strange, subnormal creations of Erskine Caldwell or the degenerate Virginians who appear in *Lie Down in Darkness,* a later novel in this tradition.

If it be argued that these are special cases of plague spots which novelists, by reporting, will help to remove, what shall we say of the business civilization to which, according to the dicta of the courts, the psychology of Adam Smith is to bring happiness? The novelists do not agree with the judges. The thoughtful reader has his choice among Curtis Jadwin of Frank Norris' *The Pit,* who embraces business like a bride and almost loses his wife; Robert Herrick's cynical *Memoirs of an American Citizen;* Theo-

1 "The Lower Depths," *Time,* LIV (September 12, 1949), 106.

dore Dreiser's Frank Cowperwood, whose enormous appetite for female flesh not even three volumes and a grandiose business career can satisfy; the unlovely J. Ward Morehouse in the *U.S.A.* of John Dos Passos; or the pathetic Gatsby in Fitzgerald's novel of that name, who, following the Benjamin Franklin formula for success, never wins his heart's desire. Business in Booth Tarkington's *The Turmoil* corrupts domestic happiness, as it does in Sherwood Anderson's *Marching Men,* in Sinclair Lewis's *Babbitt,* in Marquand's *H. M. Pulham, Esquire,* in O'Hara's *Appointment in Samarra.* There seems to be no connection between business and happiness in either Henry James or Edith Wharton; and, after studying the unfortunate impact of business upon the pioneer in her earlier novels, Willa Cather, most classical of recent fictionists, fled in imagination to forgotten Pueblo cultures, to Catholic enterprise in New Mexico, to French colonizing in seventeenth-century Canada.

Doubtless the truth lies somewhere between the Christmas tree glitter of the magazines and the inspissated gloom of serious fiction, but I find two reports on the situation that are sufficiently disturbing. When Robert and Helen Lynd brought out *Middletown in Transition* in 1937, sequel to *Middletown* a dozen years earlier, they found that all of Middletown operates on the assumption that the roots of living lie in the acquision of money, partly because money-mindedness is necessarily produced by the abundance of gadgets invented by American technology. Though the note of Middletown was, they said, "Forward!";[1] though their research workers found a higher proportion of smiling faces on the streets of Middletown than they saw in New York; though Middletown parents

[1] Robert S. Lynd and Helen Merrell Lynd, *Middletown in Transition: A Study in Cultural Conflicts* (New York: Harcourt, Brace and Company, 1937), p. 14.

wanted their children to have an easier time than father and mother had had, the report nevertheless concluded that men in Middletown worked, not to gain leisure as Jefferson did, but to get ahead, that the tendencies of this culture are masochistic, that the workingman clung to the notion that if you have a job, you're lucky, and that

> it is difficult for a man in such a culture to draw a line under his possessions at any point, summate them, and say, 'Here I rest. I will strive to add no more'.[1]

My other exhibit is by John Maynard Keynes, who in 1926, in *The End of Laissez-Faire,* virtually declared the end of the profit-motive theory of the pursuit of happiness, and who, according to his biographer, thus expressed himself:

> In Europe, or at least in some parts of Europe but not, I think, in the United States of America—there is a latent reaction somewhat widespread, against basing society to the extent that we do upon fostering, encouraging, and protecting the money-motives of individuals. Most religions and most philosophies deprecate, to say the least of it, a way of life mainly influenced by considerations of personal money profit. On the other hand, most men to-day reject ascetic notions and do not doubt the real advantages of wealth. Moreover, it seems obvious to them that one cannot do without the money-motive, and that apart from certain admitted abuses, it does its job well . . . Material poverty provides the incentive to change precisely in situations where there is very little margin for experiments. Material prosperity removes the incentive just when it might be safe to take a chance. Europe lacks the means, America the will, to make a move. We need a new set of convictions which spring naturally from a candid examination of our own inner feelings in relation to outside facts.[2]

[1] The same, p. 247, n. 6.

[2] Quoted in R. F. Harrod, *The Life of John Maynard Keynes* (New York: Harcourt, Brace and Company, 1951), pp. 356-357.

I am not assuming the validity of Keynesian economic theory in quoting this shrewd and sensitive observer, but I am interested to see in his statement a rationalization of the reports which American writers bring us about the state of the national happiness. They, too, seem to demand a "candid examination of our inner feelings in relation to outside facts."

iii

In discussing William James I said that the appearance of *Principles of Psychology* in 1890 marks a turning point. Happiness, decisions of the courts to the contrary notwithstanding, has been transferred from the sphere of law to the sphere of psychology. Not the public life of political science and economics, but the inner life of impulse and emotion—here in the twentieth century, most Americans seem to agree, is the sphere of felicity. James began, the American translations of Freud and Jung and American interest in such Europeans as Nietzsche, Strindberg, Wedekind, Proust, and Joyce continued, the steady transplanting of the roots of happiness out of the world of Adam Smith and Benjamin Franklin into the world of the doctor, the psychiatrist, the personnel director, and the social psychologist. It is they who have bridged the gap between the outer and the inner world, who have made the "candid examination of our inner feelings in relation to outside facts" that Keynes desires. In their hands the ancient doctrine that happiness means living in accordance with nature has taken a new form.

Nature is no longer the majestic deity of the Stoics nor the impressive world-machine of Newton, nor even the terrifying, yet tragic, nature of Tennyson, Darwin, and Thomas Hardy; nature is, on the contrary, Dionysiac, instinctive, primal; and the problem of happiness is the problem of adjustment between the primitive subliminal urges of our hidden selves and the drab and practical necessities of every day. In a general sense, modern art moves one way, expressing our primary natures, and industrial society moves in exactly the opposite way, disciplining, confining, and frustrating them. At the opening of the twenties Kenneth MacGowan expressed the philosophy of a whole generation of writers, dramatists, painters, dancers, and other artists when he said, in a book on the theater:

> Psychoanalysis, tracing back our thoughts and actions into fundamental impulses, has done more than any one factor to make us recover the sense of our unity with the dumb, mysterious processes of nature. We know now through science what the Greeks and all primitive peoples knew through instinct.[1]

The man on the street might know nothing about Dionysus and little about instinct, but the disastrous prohibition experiment showed him the vast discrepancy between law and conduct. The problem of adjusting emotional drive and outward circumstance has ever since been central to the contemporary practice of happiness, so much so that even the comic strips now include psychiatrists among their casts of characters.

The pursuit of happiness as justment goes forward on two levels: the scientific and the popular. In 1900 Jacques Loeb published his *Comparative Physiology of the Brain,* a fundamental document in behavioristic psychology; in 1909 American specialists were made aware of Pavlov's *The Orientation of the Dog to Sound;* in 1917 V. M. Bekhterev's *General Principles of Human Reflexology*[2] appeared; in 1919 John B. Watson brought out *Psychology*

[1] Kenneth MacGowan, *The Theatre of Tomorrow* (New York, 1921), p. 264.

[2] Not available to specialists until the American translation of the 1928 edition, which appeared in 1932.

from the Standpoint of a Behaviorist; and in 1920 his *Behaviorism* codified the stimulus-response theory of motive and action. Meanwhile, from 1901 to 1910 a courageous American publisher, Davis of Philadelphia, had published at intervals Havelock Ellis' classic *Studies in the Psychology of Sex;* and it is a mark of cultural change that this work, once prosecuted as obscene, was republished in 1936 in the ordinary way by the Modern Library. In 1909 the famous psychological symposium at Clark University began the vogue of Freud; in 1910 A. A. Brill published his paper on Freud's interpretation of dreams and in 1913 brought out the first of his many translations of Freud; and by 1915 Max Eastman printed in *Everybody's Magazine*[1] a popular article called "Exploring the Soul and Healing the Body." Eastman was concerned with the "magic" of dream interpretation as therapy and as a means for uncovering the unconscious. By 1920 G. Stanley Hall produced his version of Freud's *General Introduction to Psychoanalysis,* and in the twenties Greenwich Village was babbling of the libido, the id, and suppressed desires.[2] A third basic element was added in 1908 when Clifford W. Beers wrote his classic *A Mind That Found Itself,* revelations of the treatment of the insane, which led to the founding of a national association for mental hygiene. These are but three strands of an immense web.

Today the psychological approach is so commonplace that students of Ernest R. Groves and Phyllis Blanchard's *Introduction to Mental Hygiene* (1930), in the American Social Science series, read without surprise a table of con-

[1] Max Eastman, "Exploring the Soul and Healing the Body," *Everybody's Magazine,* XXXII, pp. 741-750, June, 1915. This was followed by "Mr. — er — er — oh! what's his name?" *Everybody's Magazine,* XXXIII, pp. 95-103, July, 1915.

[2] Susan Glaspell's amusing one-act satire, *Suppressed Desires,* dates from 1914.

tents which connects mental hygiene not merely with childhood, adolescence, marriage, and the like, but also with schools, the colleges, business, industry, recreation, religion, the "mental hygiene aspects of literature," and public opinion. In the last chapter, on "The Larger Aspects of Mental Hygiene," one finds that

> Mental hygiene is the application of science in an effort to help men, women, and children make sane adjustments. It recognizes the biological meaning of adaptation to environment . . . It frankly seeks personal and social happiness in the belief that this normally follows wholesome adjustment.[1]

The bibliography of a standard textbook, Fred McKinney's *The Psychology of Personal Adjustment* runs to 1390 titles. For this author:

> Happy is the man who can satisfy the basic motives of life, whose bed feels good to him after physical work or play, who looks forward to his meals, enjoys his work no matter how obscure, who appreciates the minor changes and adventures in his life—a moonlit night, strains of music, a beautiful tree in a neatly clipped lawn, burning leaves, sunrises, or even a new route home from work . . . His happiness is a by-product . . . and is not achieved through the pursuit of thrills.[2]

One cannot reasonably quarrel with this statement, but it is remote, indeed, from the world of Jefferson and Adam Smith.

The world of Jefferson and Adam Smith, in the United States at least, has indeed become the world of Adler, Jung, and Freud. The United States is today a psychological problem. In the last half-century psychological

[1] Ernest R. Groves and Phyllis Blanchard, *Introduction to Mental Hygiene* (American Social Science Series, New York, 1930), p. 454.

[2] Fred McKinney, *Psychology of Personal Adjustment* (2nd. ed.; New York: John Wiley and Sons, 1949), p. 669.

journals have multiplied; departments of psychology have advanced from minor place to major importance in the university world; the psychoanalyst has passed beyond the status of fashion into the status of expert witness in criminal trials; psychiatrists are accredited members of medical schools, hospital staffs, settlement houses, and government rehabilitation projects; psychological tests and measurements are as commonplace as testimonial letters and certificates of morality once were; and social workers, divorce courts, judges facing juvenile delinquents, army officers, navy boards, schoolteachers, and on occasion, ministers, priests, and rabbis turn as a matter of course to the psychological expert for aid, counsel, prophecy, and advice. The psychologist has taken over many of the functions of the colonial clergyman, and instructs not only individuals but groups, cities, and even the nation in modes of behavior. In this last activity, he has been joined by the sociologist and the cultural anthropologist.

Whatever doctrinal differences may divide American psychologists—and these are many—two observations may be made on their prodigious activity. The first is that the practical aim of much of their professional work is to induce what is known as "adjustment," or a harmonious (and therefore happy) relation between the inner world of the psyche and the outer world of reality, whether the clinical problem arise out of maldevelopment, domestic tension, or the strain upon the personality of the whole social order. Inasmuch as human beings do not seek out a psychologist for therapeutic purposes unless they are, as Locke would say, "uneasy," life in the United States appears to be a problem of insecurity. The child is "insecure" in its primary emotional contexts; the adolescent is "insecure" vis à vis the family, the group, or the community; the young husband or bride is "insecure" in the sexual relation; the businessman and his wife (more rarely the laborer and his helpmate) are "insecure" in a variety of ways; and most pathetic of all, the aged are "insecure" because they are "not wanted." Religion, which once seemed an emotional sheet-anchor to windward, offers small comfort to these disturbed personalities; and the "home," pictured by nineteenth-century writers as a lesser heaven, becomes either a kind of amateur snake-pit or a space unit in an apartment house, a television set, or the outlet of street-corner society. The happy agrarian republic dreamed of by Franklin and Jefferson is in this light neither happy nor agrarian nor a republic. One mournful glimpse into social change comes from the advertising of insurance and annuity companies. In less complicated societies the aged achieved status as the grandmothers, the elder statesmen, or other representatives of antique wisdom; today, one such advertisement offers $200 a month and the opportunity "to do the things I've always dreamed of doing—golf, fish, laze around a beach somewhere." The lost Atlantis of youth is scarcely thus to be revisited, and the implication that the insured has spent a life-time doing what he did *not* want to do is not reassuring.

The second general observation is that as diagnostic techniques improve, the percentage of potential or actual psychotics in the total population seems steadily to rise. Our insane asylums are filled during a period when they are understaffed and inadequately equipped, private institutions cannot care for all the others, and the increase in practicing psychoanalyists and psychiatrists naturally uncovers an increased number of psychotic personalities not sufficiently disturbed to demand institutional care but sufficiently off-balance to add to the general impression of unhappiness. Whether the present level of felicity is higher or lower than that of yesteryear there is no way of ascertaining, just as there is no way of ascertaining whether unhappiness in the United States is greater or less than unhappiness in the Scandinavias, the British Isles, or China. Much is made by some theorists of the stresses of modern living; and certain it is that what used to be called "New-Yorkitis" has developed or degenerated into the neuroses of fear, war, and the bomb. As it is fashionable in more serious literary circles to be more aware of the world of the psychoanalyist than, let us say, the world of the botanist, the chemist, or the astronomer, advanced writers are naturally persuaded that their deeper insight is justified by science, speak glibly of a tragic age, and seek escape from "guilt complexes" by rushing into anti-intellectualism. The literary mystagogue has, however, his diverting parallels with the Byronism of the nineteenth century, when the unsatisfactory conditions of a then modern age also concentrated attention upon the self.

Against these considerations others should be set. In the first place, psychology helps or cures the disturbed person in a significant number of cases and sends him back to society a happier individual. In the second place, whatever their abuses, psychological tests and measurements have kept many a square peg out of a round hole; and though alarmists may speculate as to whether the end result is to be a brave new world by 1984, human relations (and therefore social and industrial relations in an industrial society) do, in the long run, improve. In the third place, the maladjusted who come before the psychoanalysts are not necessarily a cross-section either of Americans or of American life. Equally to be considered are the holiday crowds, the millions of out-door vacationists, the crowded beaches, the national parks, the Christmas season, the national passion for baseball, our delight in gadgets, the obvious kindliness of Americans, and a thousand other components of the "American way" which do not appear in novels of tension or in discussions of sexual perversion. Against the twisted personalities who furnish too large a proportion of current books should be set the garage mechanic or the industrial chemist with, characteristically, small interest in books or in the neurotic personality of our time. This is not to say that mechanics and chemists are *per se* happy, but it raises the question: who or what represents an age. If ours is an age of anxiety, it is also the age of the engineer, that hard-headed and sometimes unenlightened character who, nevertheless, has probably done more for general happiness in the way of creature comforts, the practical solution of sociological problems, and a kind of extroverted valuation than has any other human product of the age of specialization.

iv

In a recent number of *The Nation* there appeared a small and discreet advertisement headed: "exit loneliness," the body of which read: "Somewhere there is someone you would like to know. Somewhere there is someone, who would like to know you. We can help you find a richer, happier life through discreet, dignified social introduction." If happiness in the twentieth century has become a problem of adjustment, that problem passes out of the hands of psychological specialists into the great, broad, hearty domain of popular life. The advice to the love-lorn column, the prestige of names like Dorothy Dix and Mary Hayworth, the vogue of departments like "The Tower Room" in the *Woman's Home Companion* are as characteristic of the pursuit of happiness today as is the psychiatric clinic. Unfortunately there seems to be no expert analysis of the domestic advice column, theoretically written by a woman, the clientèle of which is mainly, though not uniformly, feminine. Love, marriage, and domestic relationships are the stock-in-trade of these departments; and a little steady reading in them throws some light on the problem of happiness as adjustment at what, in the Latin sense, is the vulgar level of appeal. Students of mine who have analyzed this variety of pursuing happiness (or at least, of advising others how to pursue and secure happiness and safety) come up with some surprising glimpses into our folkways.

It is, for example, generally assumed in these columns that the individual may not alter his environment importantly. Human life is governed by general conditions which narrowly limit the sphere of the individual. The columnist sympathizes with romantic love, but takes on the whole a dim view of its future. Marriage is seldom or never discussed in terms of romantic idealism—Antony and Cleopatra and Tristan and Isolde are a couple of light years away from the columnist—but is, instead, a problem in *Gemütlichkeit*. The smooth running of the household does more for happiness than any amount of romance. "Honor" rates high (the columnist turns a severe face against two-timing) and "drunkenness" is sternly condemned (this in the land of the cocktail!). How to live well on a low income is a recurrent problem. Marriage is a "job"; it is particularly the job of the housewife and mother, who, in the best Victorian fashion, is counseled against nagging and the direct attack (except in high moments of family welfare), and is frequently advised by indirections to find direction out. One odd paradox is that an ambitious materialism ("keeping up with the Joneses") flourishes cheek-by-jowl with the belief that the best things in life are free. Although the area of individual choice is narrowly circumscribed, within this area an energizing dynamism is possible to almost anybody with the will to achieve. What is to be achieved is, for most "contributors," normality. The truth that normality cannot be defined in exact terms does not prevent the anxious young mother from desiring her children to be "normal," a desire which brings us back by a long sweep to the problem of popularity.

So far as these columns and departments center upon the "woman problem" as distinct from the general domestic issue, health, both physical and mental, beauty, and "integrity" are central. Exercises for the body and for the brain are regularly available to the inquirer. Integrity involves delicate questions of social adjustment, sometimes in the sphere of love, sometimes in the sphere of loneliness. The standard formula is that most women can easily obtain men if they work it right, but they must please and "adjust" to do so, since, apparently, the lordly male, though he comes in for some digs, remains to the end lordly. As for beauty, the accent is on youth. Not character but personality is the be-all and the end-all of "charm." However, health, possibly to avoid any sectarian issue, is seldom conceived in terms of sin versus salvation. Indeed, philosophy rather than religion is made central to "right living." The columnist sometimes attacks happiness as an aim in itself, since this is supposed to involve selfishness, and is likely to preach that happiness consists in improvement rather than resignation to the universe.

Advising women on problems of domesticity and happiness is no new thing in American life—Harriet Beecher Stowe, for example, did something of this sort many years ago—but the popular conception of happiness as adjustment has received a powerful impetus from the vogue of these newspaper and magazine features. So, likewise, a whole library of popular manuals of psychology has in the last half-century strengthened this particular philosophy of happiness; and to examine some of these books is to discover how far we have drifted from either the Horatian, the Stoic, or the Christian doctrine of happiness as resignation. Here, for example, are some ten manuals published in the second, third, and fourth decades of the present century.

In 1913 the once celebrated Horace Fletcher produced *Happiness as Found in Forethought minus Fearthought.* Assuming that "the normal condition of man in civilized life is . . . happiness," Fletcher inquired why, when "the vital truths underlying the philosophy of life" can be "intelligently stated in a few hundred words," unhappiness prevails. The cause is "weak habit-of-thought," he says, and the remedy "good habit-of-thought," which develops "appreciation." This leads to "habit-of-feeling," this to "habit-of-action," and this to happiness. Q.E.D.[1]

In 1913 also appeared *The Joys of Living* by Orison Swett Marden, a confused and shallow book, which nevertheless starts from the Dionysiac principle:

> The first duty we owe a child is to teach him to fling out his inborn gladness and joy with the same freedom and abandon as the bobolink does when it makes the meadow joyous with its song. Suppression of the fun-loving nature of the child means the suppression of its mental and moral faculties.

Later Marden says:

> If you desire to get force and vigor into your efforts, you must have a free avenue of self-expression.

The country is full of "nervous wrecks," who failed to follow the useful psychological law:

> What else in life is more valuable than the art of forgetting, of burying, covering up the disagreeable, everything that has caused us pain and hindered our progress?[2]

[1] Horace Fletcher, *Happiness as Found in Forethought minus Fearthought* (New York, 1913) pp. 1, 7, 19-20.

[2] Orison Swett Marden, *The Joys of Living* (New York, 1913), pp. 55, 106, 239.

Marden has evidently stumbled upon and misinterpreted three cardinal ideas: the dangers of frustration, the importance of self-expression, and the need of purgation through analysis. A series of sentimentalized case studies in Robert S. Carroll's *Our Nervous Friends,* 1919, seemed to support him.

Somewhat more imposing is *Outwitting Our Nerves* (1921), "a primer of psychotherapy" by Josephine A. Jackson and Helen M. Salisbury, dedicated to the proposition that "a nervous symptom [is] an unsettled ethical struggle" and that "a neurosis is a confidence game that we play on ourselves."[1] By 1929, in *Intelligent Living,* Austen Fox Riggs was disturbed by the flood of amateur books on psychology promising relief from unhappiness by remedies ranging from dietary reforms to memory culture and from posture to prayer; he set up as a norm this statement:

> A well-balanced, purposeful life is the unit of progressive civilization, and is, furthermore, a healthy life, a happy life, and all things being equal, a long life.[2]

Simultaneously, in *The Psychology of Happiness,* Walter B. Pitkin was declaring that philosophies and religions

> which have . . . taught self-denial, self-repression, a killing of the personal will, a surrender to . . . Fate or Nature or the Gods . . . mild contentment or resignation or the apathy of despair . . . are all wrong . . . all befuddled . . . We know today that happy living can be attained by at least six or seven people out of every ten, simply by right education, the right organization of personal effort, and the right selection of one's work and environment.

Happiness is nothing more than

> the emotional phase of the smooth functioning of the

[1] Josephine A. Jackson and Helen M. Salisbury, *Outwitting Our Nerves: A Primer of Psychotherapy* (New York, 1921), pp. 177, 179.

[2] Austen Fox Riggs, *Intelligent Living* (New York, 1929), p. 230.

entire organism, in which our minds and muscles carry out to a neat success the whole system of desires active at a given moment . . . the emotional tone accompanying the self-realization of a personality.[1]

Apparently the self-realization of a personality was not thus statistically evident to either Dora or Bertrand Russell in the same period. I quote from the latter's *The Conquest of Happiness* (1930):

> Though the kinds are different, you will find that unhappiness meets you everywhere . . . Stand in a busy street during working hours, or on a main thoroughfare at a week-end, or at a dance of an evening; empty your mind of your own ego, and let the personalities of the strangers about you take possession of you . . . You will find that each of these different crowds has its own trouble. In the work-hour crowd you will see anxiety, excessive concentration, dyspepsia, lack of interest in anything but the struggle . . . On a main road at the week-end, you will see men and women, all comfortably off, and some very rich, engaged in the pursuit of pleasure. This pursuit is conducted . . . at a uniform pace, that of the slowest car in the procession; it is impossible to see the road for the cars, or the scenery since looking aside would cause an accident; all the occupants of all the cars are absorbed in the desire to pass other cars . . . Or again, watch people at a gay evening. All come determined to be happy, with the kind of grim resolve with which one determines not to make a fuss at the dentist's. It is held that drink and petting are the gateways to joy, so people get drunk quickly, and try not to notice how much their partners disgust them.[2]

This Swiftian world is created, according to the philosopher, out of boredom and excitement, fatigue, envy,

[1] Walter B. Pitkin, *The Psychology of Happiness* (New York, 1929), pp. 1, 392.

[2] Bertrand Russell, *The Conquest of Happiness* (London, 1930), pp. 15-16. Lord Russell restated his view in "The American Way (A Briton Says) Is Dour," *The New York Times Magazine*, June 15, 1952, pp. 12 ff.

the sense of sin, a persecution mania, the fear of public opinion, and three kinds of self-absorption: the guilt complex, narcissism, and megalomania.

Not unnaturally, perhaps, Josephine L. Rathbone published in 1943 a book for adults entitled *Relaxation,* and Marie Beynon Ray a volume entitled *How Never To Be Tired* (1944). I pass over these, however, to call attention to *Why Be Shy?* by Louis E. Bisch (1941), the dedication of which has an interest all its own:

> To and FOR Those whose awareness of self—with its probable fears, timidities, inferiority convictions, lack of self-confidence and poise; with its defeatism and frustrations in general—has rendered their lives a puzzling problem, a downright failure, or a veritable nightmare. Those who have not yet come to realize that, behind shyness, there lie potential superiorities and the power for unsuspected achievements. Those whose cultural assets and fine inner qualities—so characteristic of the shy—place them in civilization's forefront.

If any among you are unhappy because of shyness, Bisch's conclusion should comfort you: First four conquering steps: You faced your fears; you removed your guilt; you touched up your ego; you released your abilities; all important fifth step: you turned your shyness into an asset. "Act as though the other person is shier than you."[1]

If we are to believe the *Literary Digest,* a Washington, D.C., church in 1928 turned happiness into an assembly-line problem. In a "life-adjustment clinic,"

> after the physician has regulated the body of the patient to the best of his ability the individual will be passed along to the psychiatrist, who will probe into those subtle . . . experiences which . . . have such a profound effect on the life and habits of the individual. In addition there will be social workers to deal with the present environment. Last

[1] Louis E. Bisch, *Why Be Shy?* (New York, 1941), pp. v, 265.

> of all, but perhaps most important, will come the diagnoses of the individual's religious problems and the application of the curative forces of religion.[1]

In February 1931 the *Ladies' Home Journal,* in order to make women happier, found it profitable to establish a column conducted by Dr. Karl Menninger. The editors denied that unhappiness is principally caused by fate, circumstance, or environment, and declared:

> The mental-hygiene movement is based upon scientific knowledge, research, discoveries. Unfortunately it is far from omniscient. There are problems of unhappiness which all our present knowledge cannot help. But there are many others which certainly can be untangled, and often all that is needed is a suggestion . . .[2]

The first three cases dealt with a jealous sister, a husband suffering from melancholia, and a Cuban girl who thinks only of "home, school, and marriage." Dr. Menninger did not find these interests unnatural.

Here is a characteristic article in the *Woman's Home Companion* (1937), "Getting an Early Start on Happiness." Mistaken people believe the legend that happiness is an act of God,

> but psychology improves on the legend by showing us that happiness may be sought and found in any place, because it is in ourselves that it exists and only there. Happiness is . . . an individual product; it depends upon the chemistry of our hormones, the organization and health of the body's cells, the stability of the nervous system, the attitudes of the mind . . . As such, it may be learned.[3]

[1] "A Life-Adjustment Clinic," *The Literary Digest* (from the *Ladies' Home Journal),* XCIX (December 8, 1928), p. 30.

[2] Karl Menninger, "Mental Hygiene in the Home: Unhappiness," *Ladies' Home Journal,* XLVIII (February 1931), 96.

[3] Lorine Pruette, "Getting an Early Start on Happiness," *Woman's Home Companion,* LXIV (January 1937), 9.

Statistics show, declared *School and Society* in 1942, that

> one out of each 16 individuals now in our educational systems over this vast country will fail to achieve that complete emotional state of mature adjustment which we call normal, and the resulting breakdowns indicate the need of a "program of prevention," which would embrace "social, economic, health, educational, emotional, and mental development factors."[1]

This is nothing if not generous. *The Rotarian* proclaimed in December 1949 that "happiness is an act of will, a free decision to put an end to vain regrets and vain wishes"; and in 1950, in that magazine, Will Durant spelled out this program of voluntarism: pessimism is not a philosophy but an illness; the glands, in pleasure, pour their juices into the blood; our strongest desires are rooted in instinct; and the will can harmonize the instincts.[2]

My final exhibit in this realm of the national psychology is "A 10-Day Plan for Happiness," by Luther Conant, Jr., in the *Woman's Home Companion* for October 1950. The preface is somewhat remarkable:

> Psychiatrists recognize monotony as a malady that should be promptly treated. Here is a ten-day plan—approved by them—to combat it. Actually, as the experts would tell you, that lost feeling—those Sunday afternoon blues—can't be blamed on your hard or boring life. It's all in your head. What you need is scientific guidance to help you regain true perspective and start living life fully again. This ten-day plan does that. Its simple psychology should work for you. All that's demanded is that you give it the same fair test that you would give a ten-day reducing diet.

[1] "Mental Healing Seen as the Need of the Age," *School and Society*, LVI (December 5, 1942), 557. This is an account of an address delivered by Marion E. Kenworthy, "Let Us Throw Off the Shackles of Fear."

[2] André Maurois, "Happiness Is a State of Mind," *The Rotarian*, LXXV (December 1949), 9; Will Durant, "What Makes Men Happy," *The Rotarian*, LXXVII (November 1950), 8-11.

V

We have come a long way from that spring day in Williamsburg in 1776 when Colonel Archibald Cary presented his committee report on a declaration of rights, including the right to pursue happiness. The semantic shift in the meaning of "happiness" in this interval parallels the semantic change in the meaning of "commerce," but unlike the case of commerce clause, the courts have failed to recognize the twentieth-century meaning of happiness as adjustment. If unhappiness is the product of faulty hormones, buried psychic traumas, a childhood psychologically unsatisfactory, and a complex of unfortunate personal relationships, the elite are no more shielded from misfortune than any other social group—are, indeed, in some sense, more vulnerable to unhappiness than many others. Consequently, the comfortable assumption that the spectator theory of happiness, pleasant enough for the gentry, is the national norm falls to the ground; and in some sense happiness becomes a problem in *expertise*. The country gentlemen and the merchant prince descend; the child psychologist, the doctor, the psychiatrist, and the personnel director take their places. George Mason's phrase guaranteed to the people the right to pursue and obtain happiness and safety. Whatever is meant by happiness, the twentieth-century has interpreted "safety" as "security," security meaning not only job-tenure, sickness benefits, unemployment insurance, and social security, but also security in the psychiatric sense, as when we say of a child, he doesn't feel "secure" in relation to his psychological environment. The phrase, "the age of anxiety," refers not only to the fear of genocide following upon atomic warfare, it refers also to the widespread sense of psychic insecurity uncovered by investigators and dramatized by novelists, poets, and playwrights. In some sense, the norm of happiness being no longer determined by an elite (of whom Mason and Jefferson were characteristic), one can say that the concept of happiness has been democratized in proportion as the causes of unhappiness have been popularized, but that this concept has not yet acquired legal or constitutional force.

The continuing element in most of the definitions of happiness we have examined has been physical health, often considered the basis of mental well-being. If the American people decide that the theory of happiness as adjustment is paramount, they may profoundly alter constitutional theory and legal practice. For example, the opposition of the American Medical Association to socialized medicine rests in large degree upon two traditional doctrines: a philosophy of individualism and laissez-faire economic theory. If happiness can be pursued and obtained only with the aid of the physician and the psychiatrist, however, the individualistic attitude of the physicians could conceivably be over-ridden by an appeal to the constitutional right of pursuing happiness, so far as this appears in state constitutions and so far as the Declaration of Independence is used by the courts to construe constitutional theory. It is also theoretically conceivable that the whole basis of our public school system might be radically shifted, should we be nationally persuaded that adjustment in childhood is a *sine qua non* of happiness. In a third area, it is evident that industrial civilization has produced, as an unexpected by-product, an embarrassing amount of leisure. On the one hand, the political theory which permits government, state or national, to set aside national and state areas as playgrounds and recreation centers for the happiness of the people might be indefinitely extended; on the other hand, if leisure means monotony, and if monotony is, indeed, a "malady that should be promptly treated," it is again theoretically possible that institutional therapy for the disordered or the insane will seem to be costly and unnecessary in greater or less degree, if, through the management of leisure under proper guidance, abnormal tendencies can be discovered, checked, and remedied in time to prevent the need of institutional care.

These are, indeed, but guesses—three or four out of many that suggest themselves. Up to the present, legal damatization of the unalienable right to pursue happiness has had but a small and unimportant role in the courts. I venture to speculate upon the potentialities of the phrase by suggesting that these potentialities are today as great and dramatic as were the potentialities, since realized, in the commerce clause or in due process of law. Should these potentialities turn into use, conservatives are likely to declare that happiness has, indeed, become no laughing matter, and liberals will probably rejoice that the intangible goods of life, such as happiness, serenity, and emotional balance are being more fairly distributed among the inhabitants of the United States. The agrarian republic has vanished. Can this industrial empire distribute happiness in equal portions among mankind?

Everything will turn, it seems to me, on the question whether happiness is construed in modern America as primarily an individual or primarily a social state. The difficulty in the current concept of the term—happiness as adjustment—is that all the emphasis is laid upon the inner life, outer facts being so essentially hostile that the utmost attainment of the psyche is a kind of uneasy truce with a sleepless enemy. The difficulty, on the other hand, in happiness as a social goal is not only that it is impossible to make others happy against their will, but also that it opens the door to every variety of social meddling.

Perhaps the very word is unfortunate. Obviously the eighteenth-century men did not mean by happiness that wholly emotional and transient euphoria connoted by wedding parties, love affairs, skiing, and the endless pursuit of thrills. They had in mind not so much happiness as contentment; and if their concept of content was to our taste overly colored with a melancholy resignation, there is no essential logic whereby the doctrine of contentment has to be gray. It may be that Jefferson was wiser than are we, and that to rest content with limited, yet not unsatisfactory, opportunities and powers is the highest felicity an individual or a nation can achieve in an indifferent universe.

Table of Cases